THE FALL OF COMMUNISM

1989: The Year the World Changed

by Jeffrey B. Symynkywicz

Dillon Press • Parsippany, New Jersey

For Micah, with great pride and much joy

Credits
Cover: The Bettmann Archive

AP/Wide World Photos: 12, 15, 31, 40, 44, 69, 73, 102, 105. The Bettmann
Archive: 28, 46, 55, 59, 66, 97, 129. Liaison International/Abe Ajansi: 86;
Forrest Anderson: 51; Eric Bouvet: 92; KOK: 19; G. Merillon/P. Piel: 75;
Merillon-Vioujard: 108; Novosti: 36; Paul O'Driscoll: 23; William Stevens:
119; Anthony Suau: 79; Weco: 111. Sovfoto/Eastfoto: 84, 126.
Map by Ortelius Design: 6.

Library of Congress Cataloging-in-Publication Data
Symynkywicz, Jeffrey.
  1989: the year the world changed / by Jeffrey B. Symynkywicz.
    p. cm. — (The fall of communism)
    Includes bibliographical references and index.
    ISBN 0-87518-631-9 — ISBN 0-382-39191-8 (pbk.)
    1. Europe, Eastern—Politics and government—1989—Juvenile literature.
  2. China—History—Tiananmen Square Incident, 1989—Juvenile literature.
  [1. Europe, Eastern—Politics and government—1989. 2. China—
History—Tiananmen Square Incident, 1989.] I. Title.
DJK51.S96 1996
947.085—dc20   95-14703

Summary: A survey of the momentus events of the year 1989 in the
Communist states of Eastern Europe, the Soviet Union, and the People's
Republic of China, with historical background and discussion of the outlook
for the future.

 Published by Dillon Press,
A Division of Simon & Schuster
299 Jefferson Road, Parsippany, NJ 07054

First edition

Printed in the United States of America

10 9 8 7 6 5 4 3 2 1

CONTENTS

chapter 1

New Year's Day, 1989

At the stroke of midnight on January 1, 1989, as it did every night at that hour, the large iron bell of the Moscow Kremlin began to toll. Beneath the red stone walls of the mighty fortress that had come to symbolize the Soviet state and that was, in a sense, the very center of Communism, a large crowd of partygoers huddled close to one another as protection against the harsh winter cold. The temperature had been hovering at close to zero degrees Fahrenheit for most of the week. Even by the standards of a Moscow winter, this one was colder than most. Now, as the night wore on, the temperature sank even lower. A light snow began to fall, adding a powdery white layer to the heavy, dark fur and woolen coats and hats of the men and women who had assembled in Red Square to greet the New Year.

Since the founding of the Soviet state in 1917, the Communist authorities had discouraged the celebration of Christmas. As a result, New Year's Day had become the Russian people's most festive celebration. For weeks leading up to January 1, families would prepare for the holiday. Smiling pictures of Grandfather Frost, the Russian version of Santa Claus, would appear in shop windows. Gifts would be wrapped and safely tucked away. Women and men would stand in line for hours, waiting to buy the ingredients for the traditional New Year's feast.

This year, it seemed, getting ready for the holiday had been especially difficult. The most popular gift items—children's clothing and toys, perfumes and specially scented bath soaps, winter boots and women's shoes—had disappeared some time ago from store shelves. There were shortages of the food items needed to put together the holiday *zakuska* table of appetizers and snacks. Cheese, salami, canned meat, and fish were all in short supply, as were the chocolate, raisins, yeast, cottage cheese, and sour cream needed to prepare the traditional New Year's breads and cakes.

But on this New Year's Eve, people forgot about their country's problems for a while as the Kremlin's bell rang in the New Year, 1989. Men and women hugged one another and kissed and shouted for joy. All around Red Square, bottles of inexpensive Russian champagne were uncorked, and even the most discouraged offered toasts—to a new year, to hope, to the dream of a brighter future.

▼ ▲ ▼

As 1989 began, there was both hope and uncertainty around the world. In the Chinese city of Nanjing, just northwest of Shanghai, extra policemen were on duty to guard against renewed outbreaks of the student demonstrations that had marked the past several days. In the mid-1980s, Deng Xiaoping and other leaders of China's Communist government had introduced a broad program to reform their country's economic system. Although the reforms had been quite successful, and the standard of living for most Chinese people had improved as a result, students in China's large universities were forced to live as hard a life as ever. In Nanjing, several hundred students had dared to take to the streets to protest the crowded, unsafe conditions in their college dormitories and the meager food rations they received each month. Some were especially angry that foreigners studying in China, especially those from African countries, were provided with new apartments and given access

to special state food stores usually reserved for wealthy foreigners and high officials of the Communist Party. During the past month, several African students had been beaten by Chinese students, and their home countries had protested to the Chinese government. As the anti-African demonstrations grew larger, officials decided to move forcibly against the protesters. On the morning of December 31, 1988, armed policemen arrested 140 young people in connection with the anti-African protests. It had been a tense, violent day in the streets of Nanjing. But now the streets of that city, and of cities throughout the People's Republic of China, were quiet once again.

▼ ▲ ▼

In Eastern Europe, the New Year was being greeted with a wide array of feelings. In some places, where Communist governments seemed as powerful and as firmly in control as ever before, there was little hope that the future would differ in any noticeable way from the recent past.

In the German Democratic Republic, or East Germany, the Communist-led government of Erich Honecker seemed intent on tightening its grip on its citizens. Late in October 1988 one of the leading members of the Politburo of the East German Communist Party had declared that there would be no East German version of *perestroika*, the program of political and democratic reform introduced in the Soviet Union by Mikhail Gorbachev. In fact, the East German authorities had grown so fearful of the changing attitudes in the Soviet Union that they had ordered a ban on the sale of Soviet newspapers and magazines in East Germany. While men and women in capitalist West Germany could freely buy copies of newspapers and magazines from the Soviet Union, their counterparts in Communist East Germany now faced stiff fines, even imprisonment, if they were caught trying to purchase recent editions of *Pravda*, *Sputnik*, and the *Moscow News*, which were smuggled into East Germany from the USSR.

In Czechoslovakia, too, the hard-line Communist leadership seemed as strong as ever, in spite of the efforts of a small, dedicated group of human rights activists. There were, however, some hints of change within Czechoslovakia. In August 1988, in the heart of Prague, the capital, 10,000 people had gathered to remember the twentieth anniversary of the Soviet-led invasion of their country in 1968. Two months later, in October, thousands had gathered to celebrate the seventieth anniversary of Czechoslovak independence and to demand greater freedom and democracy. Then, on December 10, over 6,000 people came together once again in Wenceslas Square in Prague to commemorate the fortieth anniversary of the United Nations' Universal Declaration of Human Rights. On this occasion those gathered in the square were addressed by one of the leaders of the human rights movement in Czechoslovakia, a well-known playwright named Václav Havel. In his speech, Havel referred to the changes that were brewing. "It seems we are living in a dynamic and promising period, and our society is beginning to recover from a long slumber."[1] The crowd cheered in response. But officials in Czechoslovakia's Communist government, including President Gustav Husák and Communist Party leader Milos Jakes, insisted that they would never enter into talks with those who sought to undermine their rule.

In Bulgaria, Communist leader Todor Zhivkov also seemed determined to remain forever in the leadership position he had held since 1954. During the summer of 1988, he had succeeded in removing his chief rival for power, Chudomir Alexandrov, from the Politburo of the Bulgarian Communist Party. Alexandrov had tried to convince the party to support a program of rapid political and economic reform. Some had even dared to call him "Bulgaria's Gorbachev." Now, with Alexandrov out of the way, Zhivkov and other more traditional Communist leaders were certain that they could quickly sidetrack any further attempts at reform within Bulgaria.

Nearby, in Romania, as one year gave way to another, people seemed completely worn out and dispirited as they looked forward to another dreary winter of food shortages, insufficient fuel, and the constant surveillance of the Securitate, the security police of their dictatorial leader Nicolae Ceauşescu. When Ceauşescu had become head of Romania's Communist Party in 1965, he had been hailed by many as a reformer, a new kind of Communist. Among the leaders of the Warsaw Pact, the military alliance that bound the Communist states of Eastern Europe to the Soviet Union, he alone had forbidden the use of his country's troops in the invasion of Czechoslovakia in 1968. In 1980, he had denounced the Soviet Union's invasion of Afghanistan, and Romania was the only one of the socialist states of Eastern Europe to defy the Soviet boycott of the 1980 Olympic Games in Los Angeles. That summer the crowd at the games had cheered loudly as the athletes from the Socialist Republic of Romania had marched onto the field. Now, however, the world watched in horror as Ceauşescu, his wife, Elena, and assorted friends and relatives ran the country of Romania as if it were their personal household. Romania seemed a hopeless, desperate land as 1988 drew to a close.

▼ ▲ ▼

Elsewhere in Eastern Europe, however—in Hungary and in Poland—many of the men and women who gathered to celebrate the arrival of 1989 dared to entertain the thought that the new year might truly bring major changes. In Hungary in May 1988, Janos Kadar had stepped down as head of the Hungarian Workers' Party, as the country's Communist Party was known. Kadar was 76 years old and had led the party since 1956, a total of 32 years. He was replaced by Karoly Grosz, a much younger man who was also a great admirer of the Soviet leader Gorbachev. In spite of opposition from more traditional Communists within the party, Grosz and his supporters began

almost immediately to restructure Hungary's economic system.
Now private businesses were allowed to compete freely with
government-owned companies. A stock market was established
in Budapest, where shares of privately owned companies were
bought and sold openly. As the Hungarian economy was
reformed, people began to demand greater political freedom as
well. Soon, small alternative political groups were organized,
including the Hungarian Democratic Forum, the Alliance of
Young Democrats, and the Network of Free Initiatives.

As partygoers crowded the streets of Poland's capital,
Warsaw, on New Year's Eve, 1988, the air was filled with
rumors of major changes that might be coming Poland's way.
But the Polish refused to give themselves over to any illusion
that change could come easily and quickly. They still remembered all too clearly the exciting days of August 1980, when an
electrician named Lech Walesa had dared to lead a strike at the
huge Lenin Shipyard in Gdansk. They remembered how thousands of others had followed Walesa's lead, and how strikes had
soon spread to shipyards and factories all along Poland's
northern Baltic coast. They remembered how the Communist
government had been forced to accept the strikers' main
demands, including recognition of the right of workers to orga-
nize their own trade unions, free of the interference of the
government or the Communist Party.

The workers of Poland called their new independent trade
union Solidarity and elected Lech Walesa as their chairman. As
Solidarity's membership and influence grew, Communist officials in both Warsaw and Moscow looked upon the situation with
increasing alarm. The Soviet leader Leonid Brezhnev warned
that Soviet troops might be forced to intervene in Poland unless
Polish authorities dealt "decisively" with the threat at hand.
Early in 1981, the Polish defense minister, General Wojciech
Jaruzelski, became the country's new premier. A few months
later, at Soviet insistence, Jaruzelski was also named first secretary of the Polish Workers' (Communist) Party.

Striking Lenin Shipyard workers in Gdansk, Poland

The people of Poland remembered vividly what happened next. On December 13, 1981, General Jaruzelski announced that Poland was under martial law. The country's constitution was suspended, and the army was given direct control of the government. The Solidarity movement was declared illegal. All public meetings were prohibited. Lech Walesa and other opposition leaders were imprisoned on and off for many months over the next six years.

In spite of the banning of Solidarity, however, the serious economic problems Poland faced steadily worsened. By 1985 the country's foreign debt—the amount of money it owed to foreign banks and governments—had reached nearly $40 billion. The shelves of state-owned shops were often nearly empty, and people had to spend long hours waiting in line to purchase just the basic necessities. At the same time, an increasingly large proportion of the population was spending more and more money in the illegal but flourishing "black markets." The country faced a

severe housing shortage as well. As the nation's foreign debt
increased, the government raised prices on basic consumer
goods, such as milk, bread, and cooking oil. To meet these
higher costs, workers throughout Poland demanded higher
wages—which the cash-poor government was unable to pay.

By May of 1988, discontent with the state of the economy had
spread throughout Poland. Workers in Gdansk, where
Solidarity had been formed eight years before, went on strike.
They even dared to unfurl once again the banner of their out-
lawed movement. Openly and unafraid, they chanted the same
words they had shouted nearly a decade before: "There can be
no liberty without Solidarity."

As summer came, the wave of strikes grew even larger. The
Communist government seemed confused, unable to take any
action to stop the revolt. Many feared that Poland was on the
verge of economic collapse. Yet, publicly at least, the Communist
authorities refused even to discuss lifting the ban on Solidarity.
"The Solidarity movement belongs to the past for good,"[2] one
Polish official told representatives of the foreign press.

But behind the scenes, important changes were already
underway. On August 31, the Polish interior minister, Czeslaw
Kiszczak, met with Lech Walesa and promised that the government would enter into negotiations if Walesa would make a
public statement asking the striking workers to return to their
jobs. Between September and December 1988, negotiations were
held outside of Warsaw between government representatives and
a "Citizens Committee" composed of Walesa and other
Solidarity leaders.

The happy crowd in Warsaw's Victory Square gave a loud
roar as the ancient bell in the Cathedral of St. John began to toll
in the New Year. Toasts were made—to happiness and to the
future, to freedom and to hope. What no one knew was that by
the following spring the center of Warsaw would once again be
filled with large, excited crowds, gathered this time to celebrate
the end of one era and the beginning of another.

chapter 2

Warsaw: The Polish Round Table

The large, dark mahogany table—28 feet across when fully assembled—was the finest ever produced at the furniture factory in Henrykow. For several weeks the best workers in the plant had labored night and day to complete each of the table's 14 sections. The finely detailed work on its pedestals and along its sides recalled the superior craftmanship of an earlier age. The table was a true showpiece. All the workers in the Henrykow factory could be justifiably proud of it.

But now many doubted that the table would ever be used. The original order for it had arrived at Henrykow in late August 1988 directly from the office of the interior minister himself. The government was about to enter into negotiations with members of the opposition to find a solution to Poland's economic crisis. Round-table talks, obviously, required a round table. So representatives of the Polish government had contacted the factory at Henrykow to order a table large enough to accommodate all who would take part in the negotiations.

No time had been wasted. By the middle of October, work on the table was completed, and a special truck arrived at the furniture plant to transport the table's 14 carefully crated sections to Jablonna Palace, just outside of Warsaw. There, another group of workers unloaded the large doughnut-shaped table around which representatives from various sectors of Polish society would meet to discuss their country's future.

The table sat unused in the central hall of the Jablonna Palace for over a month. Before long, most Poles had given up hope that there would be any talks at all. At the beginning of September 1988, at the suggestion of Solidarity leader Lech Walesa, shipyard workers in Gdansk and other Polish cities had agreed to end their month-long strike. In return, Walesa had gained from Poland's Communist government the promise of a "Polish Round Table," at which representatives from through-out Poland might openly discuss the political and economic

Solidarity leader Lech Walesa addresses a large crowd of workers.

situation in the country. However, negotiations to establish ground rules for the talks stalled almost immediately.

On November 19, the increasingly impatient Solidarity leader met secretly once again with Czeslaw Kiszczak, Poland's minister of the interior, and Stanislaw Closek, secretary of the Communist Party's Central Committee. Clearly and forcefully, Walesa told them that continued talks depended, above all, on the legalization of Solidarity. If Solidarity was not legalized again, Walesa said, then there would be no round-table talks, and he would tell the workers of Gdansk to go back on strike. On hearing Walesa's demand Kiszczak and Closek stormed out of the room angrily. A few days later the large table was dismantled, put back into its shipping crates, and driven back to the factory at Henrykow. The idea of a Polish Round Table seemed finished.

Even before entering into talks with the Communist leadership, Lech Walesa had agreed to a nationally televised debate with Alfred Miodowicz, president of the government-recognized National Alliance of Trade Unions. The well-educated and polished Miodowicz was certain that he would be able to humiliate the somewhat rough and plain-spoken Walesa. He even boasted that "Mr. Walesa's weaker intellectual capacity"[1] would be no match for his own superior knowledge and command of the language.

Walesa realized that this might be his one opportunity to win over millions of his fellow Poles to Solidarity's position. A team of Solidarity supporters from various fields was assembled to coach him for the debate. On the evening of November 24, a confident Lech Walesa arrived at the studio of Poland's national television network. "I felt like a prizefighter before a championship bout," he wrote later. He even turned to Miodowicz just before the debate began and exclaimed, "I'm going to punch your lights out!"[2]

Indeed, to most observers, Walesa appeared to get the better of Miodowicz. The Solidarity chief was forceful and uncompromising as he argued for democratic change within Poland. Yet most Poles also sensed in Walesa a wisdom and maturity that, some believed, had not been there eight years before. Now he seem to exhibit a greater willingness to listen to others—even to give in on some points if need be—to usher in a new era for Poland.

Overnight, it seemed, support for the legalization of Solidarity spread throughout Polish society. The only ones now insisting that the ban on the union be maintained were certain powerful men within the Communist Party. Finally even General Jaruzelski came to believe that only negotiations could save Poland from economic collapse and that Solidarity had to be legalized once again if these negotiations ever were to take place.

On January 16, 1989, Prime Minister Mieczyslaw Rakowski recommended at a meeting of the Central Committee of the Communist Party that the ban on Solidarity be lifted. Then General Jaruzelski himself spoke forcefully in favor of Rakowski's motion. If Poland's problems were ever to be solved, Jaruzelski said, then there was a need for joint effort and compromise.

Still, many Central Committee members were not convinced. While the proposals of the party's leadership had always been obediently approved by the assembled delegates in the past, this time Rakowski's recommendations faced open opposition. There was heated discussion. Many Communists continued to resist the idea of the government entering into open and free negotiations with Lech Walesa and his associates from Solidarity—men the government had long portrayed as little more than outlaws. Finally, General Jaruzelski saw no choice but to put the full power of his presidency solidly behind the proposal to legalize Solidarity. He asked for a vote of confidence from the assembled party members. Should he lose, he said, then he and his entire government would resign, and Poland would be plunged into an even deeper political crisis.

Finally, at three o'clock in the morning on January 18, a vote was taken. By a wide margin, the Central Committee of the Polish United Workers' Party affirmed their support for the policies of General Wolclech Jaruzelski—including his recommendation to lift the ban on Solidarity.

A few days later, an official of the interior ministry placed a telephone call to the furniture plant in Henrykow. The upshot of the conversation: A truck would bring the specially ordered table back to Warsaw later that week. On the morning of February 6, 57 representatives of various Polish groups, including the government, the Communist Party, the Catholic Church, Alfred Miodowicz's National Alliance of Trade Unions, *and* Solidarity, gathered at the round table under a huge crystal chandelier in the Hall of Columns of the headquarters of the Council of Ministers.

Interior Minister Kiszczak, representing the government, spoke first. The reconstruction of the country's economy would require the support and cooperation of all Poles, Kiszczak declared. In exchange for this support, the government was willing to legalize the Solidarity movement once again and guarantee them a share of the seats in the National Assembly. Poland must not be allowed to become "the sick man of Europe," the interior minister said. There must be cooperation and compromise on the part of all the parties involved so that Poland would not again experience the "anarchy and destruction" that had marked the period of Solidarity's earlier legalization in 1980 and 1981.[3]

Walesa spoke next. He agreed that it was necessary to avoid confrontation and to make compromises. But he also insisted that if the government wanted the opposition to share in the responsibility for rebuilding Poland, then Solidarity must also be given a share of power within the government. "We know it—the country is ruined," Walesa stated. Only a system based on political and economic freedom could repair the damage that had been done, he claimed.[4]

At the conclusion of the first day's speeches, the Round Table divided into three working groups, called the Small Tables. One of these groups would consider questions of economic and social policy. Another would look at how labor unions within Poland should be organized. The third Small Table was to consider questions related to the reform of the country's political system.

The Polish government and opposition groups, including Solidarity, take part in Round Table negotiations.

Each of the three groups, in turn, was then divided into even smaller subgroups, called End Tables. Each End Table was to consider some aspect of national life: for example, questions related to education, science and technology, ecology, or health. Through the work of the Small Tables and End Tables, hundreds of men and women became involved in the negotiations of the Polish Round Table.

The opening session of the Round Table proceedings was broadcast live on Polish television. Soon, photographs of Polish government and opposition leaders sitting at the same table considering questions of the country's political and economic future appeared on the front pages of newspapers all across Europe and around the world. The image of Interior Minister Kiszczak negotiating openly with men imprisoned under his orders just a few years before became a vivid symbol of the important changes that were now taking place in Poland.

▼ ▲ ▼

After nearly two months of hard negotiating, the government and Solidarity finally reached an agreement. A new two-chambered National Assembly was to be established. In the larger lower house, or Sejm, the Communists and their allies would be guaranteed 65 percent of the seats. Solidarity would be allowed to compete in free and open elections for the remaining 35 percent. All 100 seats of the new upper house, the Senate, were to be chosen through completely free and open elections. The Senate would have the right to overturn laws passed by the Sejm.

In addition to the National Assembly, a new office, president of the republic, would be created. The president was to be elected to a single six-year term by the members of both houses of the assembly. The president's powers were to include command of the armed forces and the right to dissolve the National Assembly. It was generally assumed that General Jaruzelski would become Poland's new president.

Under the terms of the Round Table agreement, elections were scheduled for the first week in June, less than two months away. In agreeing to such major reforms in the country's political structure, Poland's Communist leaders hoped to convince the opposition, as well as world public opinion, of their sincerity in seeking genuine change. They hoped that by allowing Solidarity a substantial—though minority—share in the government, they might also be able to enlist the union's support for the difficult and painful reforms that would be needed to modernize the Polish economy. The Communists were also confident that if elections were scheduled as soon as possible after the conclusion of the Round Table talks, the party's well-established organization would prove far superior to that of Solidarity.

Solidarity leader Lech Walesa was satisfied with the accomplishments of the Polish Round Table. He had achieved all of his major objectives: legalization of Solidarity, free elections, a role in Poland's new government, and broad reforms in the Polish economy. Now there was no time to waste in preparing for the June elections. A "Citizens Committee" of Solidarity leaders was established to coordinate the campaign. A large run-down building in Warsaw was rented for the organization's headquarters. Soon, large red and white Solidarity banners were fluttering in the breeze over Victory Square, as though issuing a bold challenge to the Communists in offices across the way. The first issue of Solidarity's new "Election Gazette" (*Gazeta Wyborcza*) appeared on May 8. The Gazette was the first uncensored newspaper to appear in Poland since the Communist takeover in 1948. The next evening the first of Solidarity's political commercials was shown on Polish television.

The Communists, on the other hand, seemed confused by the prospect of having to face a free vote of the Polish people. The party had always been very effective in imposing its will on the people, but it had not competed in a genuinely free election in over 40 years. The government recruited celebrities from various fields of Polish life to stand for office as "independent" candidates. The Communists hoped that these well-known "independents"—including Poland's first cosmonaut and a widely recognized zookeeper who hosted a popular nature program on television each week—would take votes away from Solidarity and thus increase the Communist majority.

On election day, June 4, however, it quickly became obvious that the Communists' tactics had not succeeded. Only one independent candidate was elected to the Sejm: A millionaire from the northwestern Polish city of Pila, who spent huge amounts of his own money and campaigned in his own private airplane, managed to defeat the Solidarity candidate by a very narrow margin. In every one of the other districts where Solidarity was on the ballot, its candidates were victorious. Solidarity captured 161 seats in the 460-member Sejm.

Likewise, in elections for the Senate, the Solidarity candidate was defeated in only a single district. Thus the opposition gained control of 99 of the 100 seats in the assembly's upper chamber. This majority gave Solidarity the power to block any laws passed by the Communist-controlled Sejm.

The elections brought even more bad news for the Communists. Although the party's candidates had sought election to the Sejm on an uncontested list that did not include Solidarity candidates, the complicated Polish election law still required all candidates to receive a majority of the votes cast in order to be elected. The Communist-endorsed candidates thought that they would be elected easily because they were running for their seats unopposed. Many Poles, however, still refused to vote for them! Rather than using the pencils in their polling booths to check off the only names on the ballot—those of the Communist candidates—millions of men and women throughout Poland drew slashes through the names of Prime Minister Rakowski, Interior Minister Kiszczak, and other top Communist officials. When all the votes were finally counted, it was announced that 33 out of 35 of the Communists' top candidates had gone down to defeat because they had been crossed off the ballot. New candidates would have to be selected to fill their seats in the Sejm.

Solidarity's victory was complete, so complete that one of the losing candidates was heard to remark that if Solidarity had run a cow with a Solidarity banner around its neck for a seat in the Senate, the cow, no doubt, would have won easily![5] Yet some feared that Solidarity's victory was perhaps *too* complete, and the Communists' defeat too humiliating for the party to accept. Even the election of General Jaruzelski to the presidency—one of the chief assumptions behind the Round Table agreement— soon was cast in doubt. Solidarity had long looked upon

Jaruzelski as one of its most bitter opponents. It was he, after all, who had declared martial law and had banned the union in 1981. Under no circumstances could Solidarity's representatives be expected to cast their votes in favor of his election as their country's president. On the other hand, some of Solidarity's leaders feared that if Jaruzelski were denied the presidency, the Communists might find some excuse to ignore the results of the elections and cancel the entire Round Table agreement. All of their hard work then would have been for nothing.

On July 19, 1989, the members of the Sejm and Senate met in joint session to choose the president. To be elected, Jaruzelski

Poles voting in free elections in June 1989

would need a majority of the ballots cast. When their votes were combined with those of the smaller Peasant and Democratic parties, the Communists still held an overwhelming majority in the Sejm. Both the Peasants and the Democrats had been little more than puppets of the Communists since the founding of the Polish People's Republic following World War II. The Round Table had given these minor parties one fourth of the seats in the Sejm—votes that the Communists assumed they could control whenever they needed them. But now, with Solidarity's landslide victory, the political situation in Poland had changed completely. Many Peasant and Democratic representatives in the assembly announced that they would no longer follow the Communists' lead, and so would be voting against the election of Jaruzelski. The faltering Communists now seemed in danger of being swept out of power altogether.

As unbelievable as it would have seemed just a short time before, Jaruzelski's election to the presidency now depended on the cooperation of the Solidarity leadership in the Sejm and the Senate. Every time a vote was cast against the general's election, a Solidarity representative would either cast a blank ballot or leave the chamber, thus being recorded as absent from the voting. Through these complicated maneuvers, Jaruzelski was able to win election to the Polish presidency, but only by a single vote.

▼ ▲ ▼

At first, Jaruzelski seemed intent on ignoring the fact that he owed his election to Solidarity. Shortly after assuming his new office, Jaruzelski proposed that Interior Minister Kiszczak become the prime minister of the new government. However, Lech Walesa and Solidarity's other leaders refused even to consider entering into a coalition with a man whom the voters of Poland had overwhelmingly rejected just a few weeks before. Instead, Walesa appealed to the leaders of the Communists' former allies, the Peasant and Democratic parties. Together, he said, they could form a new government that would have the support of a majority of the National Assembly. On the morning of August 17, Walesa met with Roman Malinowski, head of the Peasant party, and Democratic Party leader Jerzy Jozwiak at Myslewski Palace in Warsaw. They were joined later in the day by Kiszczak himself. After several hours of tough negotiating, the four men agreed to the formation of "a government in the interests of the nation."[6]

Tadeusz Mazowiecki, a leading Solidarity journalist, was to be named Poland's new prime minister. Solidarity would also hold 11 seats in the new 23-member cabinet. The Communists would retain control of the powerful ministries of defense and the interior, as well as the ministries of agriculture and transportation. The Peasant party would have 4 posts, and the Democrats, 3. An independent professor from Posnan, Krzysztof Skubiszewski, was to be named Poland's new foreign minister.

On September 12, Tadeusz Mazowiecki, the first non-Communist prime minister of Poland in over 40 years, appeared before the National Assembly to present his cabinet and his government's program for the future of the country. The visitors' gallery was packed with spectators. Seated in places of honor were Lech Walesa and his wife, Miroslawa—or Danka, as everyone knew her. President Jaruzelski, dressed in full army uniform as always, his eyes hidden behind his ever-present dark glasses, watched from the special presidential box. Many of the Solidarity representatives wore large ribbons on their lapels, all bearing the familiar Solidarity insignia. It was a happy, festive occasion—a chance for all Poles to come together in a spirit of cooperation and national unity, a chance for those long denied a voice in their country's government to celebrate new-found freedom.

However, Mazowiecki looked tired and worn as he stood at the speaker's platform. About 45 minutes into his speech, the new prime minister's voice faltered, and he struggled for breath. Only his firm hold on the podium stopped him from falling to the ground. He was quickly led from the chamber as the audience watched in alarm. An hour later, Mazowiecki was back at the podium, joking that the long hours and stress of the past few weeks had reduced him to the same state as the Polish economy! This time he was able to finish his speech. A new age in Polish politics had begun.

Mazowiecki had just had an asthma attack, but the incident seemed to signify that Solidarity's victory would not mean that Poland's transition, either to political democracy or to economic prosperity, would be easy. The country still faced enormous challenges. Yet the Polish Round Table had served to change fundamentally the political face of Eastern and Central Europe. The Communist stranglehold on power had been broken. The era of single-party rule was over.

chapter 3

Moscow: Gorbachev and Perestroika

In March 1985, Mikhail Gorbachev succeeded Konstantin Chernenko as general secretary of the Soviet Communist Party. Almost immediately, his energetic and outspoken manner captured the imagination of people the world over and provided many Soviet citizens with a new hopefulness about the future of their country. Within a few months of coming to power, Gorbachev instituted a three-part program of openness, restructuring, and democratization aimed at reforming the Soviet Union's society, economy, and government.

Through openness, or *glasnost*, the Soviet government admitted its past crimes and mistakes and for the first time allowed historians and political scientists to question some of the basic ideas of Soviet Communism. Greater creative expression in music, literature, and the arts was permitted. Censorship of the Soviet Press was gradually lessened, though not completely eliminated.

In March 1986, a year after he had come to power, Gorbachev promised "truly revolutionary changes" in the national economy. Through his program of *perestroika*, or restructuring, steps were taken to dismantle the centralized "command system" by which all economic decisions were made by officials in Moscow. Under the new decentralized system, managers and workers in particular locations would have more control over how their plants operated and what they produced. Large government-owned collective farms and state farms would be

Muscovites walk along a new Galeries Lafayette department store. Part of Mikhail Gorbachev's program was to encourage foreign investment in Russia.

"privatized"—that is, their land would be redistributed to local farmers, who would then work together in looser, more flexible cooperatives. Foreign investment in Russia and the other Soviet republics would also be encouraged.

Gorbachev's early plans were met with a great deal of enthusiasm. However, he soon discovered that it was one thing for party congresses in Moscow to issue decrees, and another for government officials in cities and towns thousands of miles away to carry them out. A powerful group of conservatives within the party, led by the chief deputy leader Yegor Ligachev, believed that full achievement of the reforms proposed by Gorbachev would severely undermine the authority of the Soviet Communist Party. In the eyes of these dedicated Communists, Gorbachev's proposals to replace the USSR's centralized economic system with one based on a free market was nothing more than a surrender to capitalism.

Other Soviets, however, believed that Gorbachev was moving too slowly in changing the Soviet system. Chief among these more radical reformers was Boris Yeltsin. Like Gorbachev, Yeltsin had worked his way up through the Communist system. In 1986, Gorbachev had named Yeltsin secretary of the Communist Party for the city of Moscow. Soon afterward, Yeltsin was also selected for a seat on the ruling Politburo of the national party. After a little more than a year, however, Yeltsin was removed from his high posts when he openly criticized Ligachev and Gorbachev for the slow pace of *perestroika*. Especially frustrating to Yeltsin was Gorbachev's willingness to give in time and again to the demands of conservatives whenever they sought to slow the process of reform.

▼ ▲ ▼

On December 1, 1988, the Soviet legislature approved Gorbachev's plan for "democratization"—the third part of his program for remaking the Soviet Union. "There can be no

socialism without elections," Gorbachev had said. Under his
new plan, more than half of the seats in a newly created national
legislature, the Congress of People's Deputies, were to be chosen
in free elections. For the first time in Soviet history, there would
be more than one candidate on the ballot. However, there would
not be openly contested elections for every seat in the new legislature. Under Gorbachev's plan, 750 of the 2,250 delegates to
the Congress would be appointed directly by the Communist
Party and its smaller organizations.

For almost three months, an unprecedented election campaign
held the attention of people all across the Soviet Union.
Although most of the candidates were loyal members of the
Communist Party, a large number of independent candidates
also were seeking seats in the new Congress.

Among the independent candidates favoring radical reform
was Andrei Sakharov, a former Soviet nuclear scientist whom
some called the father of the Soviet Union's hydrogen bomb.
Since the early 1960s, Sakharov had been an outspoken critic of
the Communist state. For this, he was stripped of his high scientific position and placed under constant watch by the KGB, or
Committee for State Security. In 1975, Sakharov was awarded
the Nobel Peace Prize for his work in defense of human rights.
In January 1980, however, the Soviet government had forced
Sakharov to move from Moscow to Gorky, a remote city over 300
miles from the capital that foreigners were forbidden to visit.

Sakharov remained isolated in Gorky for almost seven years.
Then, late one night in December 1986, KGB agents arrived at
his apartment and installed a telephone. The next afternoon, the
telephone rang. Gorbachev was on the line. To demonstrate
publicly its sincerity in carrying out its programs of *glasnost* and
perestroika, the government had decided to allow Sakharov to
return to Moscow. "Go back to your patriotic work!"[1] the
Communist general secretary told the exiled scientist. Now, in
1989, Sakharov had been back in Moscow for more than two
years. He was as uncompromising and outspoken as ever, criti-

cizing the slow pace of Gorbachev's reforms and demanding even greater changes than the Communist general secretary proposed. As the country's first free elections in 70 years approached, Sakharov was given an excellent chance of gaining a seat in the new legislature.

So, too, was Boris Yeltsin. People in 13 different precincts all across Russia had nominated Yeltsin to stand for election. He had finally chosen to run for a seat in the Congress representing the city of Moscow. Yeltsin's opponent for the "Moscow Number One" seat was Yevgeny A. Brakov, the manager of the Moscow

Boris Yeltsin (*left*) and Andrei Sakharov ran for seats in the new legislature in the 1989 elections, the first free elections in 70 years.

factory that produced luxurious Zil automobiles for leaders of the party. While Brakov campaigned as a loyal supporter of Gorbachev and *perestroika*, voters continued to identify him with the unpopular policies of the past, under which high-ranking party members had enjoyed privileges not available to the great majority of Soviet people, such as owning the Zil automobiles that Brakov's factory produced.

Although many Soviet citizens had greeted Gorbachev's early reforms eagerly, many now felt that even after four years of *perestroika* their lives had improved little, if at all. The lines in state-owned stores were longer, and the shelves emptier, than they had been even during Leonid Brezhnev's "era of stagnation." A short poem making its way around Moscow summed up how many Soviet citizens felt:

> *Sausage prices twice as high,*
> *Where's the vodka for us to buy?*
> *All we do is sit at home,*
> *Watching Gorby drone and drone.*[2]

When Soviet voters went to the polls on March 26, they made their discontent very clear. All across the Soviet Union, radical reformers gained seats in the new legislature. Scientists within the Academy of Sciences elected the dissident Sakharov as one of their representatives. Boris Yeltsin received 89 percent of the vote in his race against Yevgeny Brakov. Historian Roy Medvedev, who had been among the first to speak out against the crimes of Stalin, was elected to the Congress, as was the famous poet Yevgeny Yevtushenko.

In the Ukraine, politicians loyal to the national Communist Party were defeated by dedicated Ukrainian nationalists. The huge victories scored by candidates who favored complete independence for the three northern Baltic republics of Lithuania, Latvia, and Estonia, which had been forcibly annexed to the USSR by Stalin in 1940, were even more threatening to the survival of the Soviet Union.

All across the country—in the three largest cities, Moscow, Leningrad, and Kiev; in Asian cities such as Alma-Ata, Yarolslavl, and Kuibyshev; even in the remote Siberian city of Tomsk—local party leaders were defeated in stunning upsets. Of 399 party officials who had run unopposed, nearly half were denied seats in the Congress when voters in their districts took the time to cross out their names on the paper ballots.

Altogether, radical reformers were victorious in 400 individual contests. Although they would still be in the minority in the 2,250-seat Congress, controlling less than one fifth of all the seats, when this bloc of independent, radical reformers chose to speak as one, their voice would certainly be heard clearly. For the first time since the Communist takeover in 1917, the Soviet government faced an organized opposition.

▼ ▲ ▼

Everywhere Gorbachev turned, it seemed, there were severe problems that demanded his attention. By the spring of 1989, nationalist demonstrations were taking place in cities all across the USSR, from the Baltic capitals in the north to the steppes of central Asia in the south. Likewise, protesters were marching in the streets of Soviet Georgia's capital, Tblisi, where, in April, security forces had killed 18 anti-Soviet demonstrators. Bloody battles raged between Armenian and Azerbaijani nationalists over control of the disputed region of Nagorno-Karabakh. There were violent clashes in parts of the western Moldavian Republic as well.

The economic situation throughout the Soviet Union also continued to worsen. The 1988 grain harvest had been the worst in three years. There was great confusion in the industrial sector. In some places, production had simply come to a halt as plant managers awaited further instructions from Moscow. Half a million coal miners in Siberia and the Ukraine were threatening to strike unless their demands for higher wages and better working conditions were met. Without a steady supply of coal, many of the largest manufacturing plants in the country would be forced to shut down.

In the midst of all these problems, the Congress of People's Deputies was called into session in Moscow on May 25, 1989. Almost from the start, the assembled delegates became entangled in bitter arguments among themselves. Gorbachev tried to use his position as chairman of the gathering to dominate the proceedings, but the newly elected radicals were not about to make things easy for him.

The debates of the Congress were televised live on Soviet television. Day after day, 200 million Soviet citizens watched as opposition deputies rose to criticize one thing after another: the slow pace of *perestroika*, the mismanagement of the economy, the continued power of high party officials, the use of deadly force against peaceful demonstrators, the 1980 invasion of Afghanistan, the continuing Soviet domination of the Baltic states. One deputy even stood to criticize the "undue influence" of Gorbachev's wife, Raisa! The government finally decided to halt continual coverage of the proceedings when large numbers of supervisors complained that their employees were getting nothing done because they were sitting almost hypnotized in front of the television, watching the latest arguments in Moscow!

In spite of loud protests from the opposition, the Congress decided to deal with only two major items of business. First, the assembled delegates would select a chairman for the legislature. Then they would choose 542 of their number as representatives to a smaller assembly, the Supreme Soviet, which would serve as the country's permanent legislature.

When it appeared as though Gorbachev would run unopposed for the position of chairman, an unknown construction engineer from a town north of Leningrad named Aleksandr Obolensky rose to nominate himself for the office. He said that he knew that he could not win, but he felt that it was important that the members of the Congress at least be given a choice in filling the most powerful office in the land. However, by a vote of 1,415 to

689, the Communist majority in the Congress decided that the election for the presidency should be limited to "serious candidates." Obolensky's candidacy would not be allowed. Gorbachev would stand for election unopposed.

The Communist majority in the Congress also overwhelmed the radical opposition when the permanent Supreme Soviet was selected. At first when the voting was completed, it appeared as though even Boris Yeltsin, by far the most popular of the opposition deputies, had not gained a seat in the permanent legislature. Yeltsin's exclusion was greeted by cries of protest from the opposition delegates, some of whom rose to denounce the "Stalinist-Brezhnevite Supreme Soviet" that was being created.

Within a few hours, thousands of citizens were rallying in front of the Congress building in Moscow, demanding that Yeltsin be seated. Thousands of men and women across the nation telephoned their delegates in Moscow or sent them telegrams, expressing their view that Yeltsin should be included on the final list of members of the Supreme Soviet. Soviet politics had never before witnessed such an outpouring of public opinion.

The Communist deputies soon realized that they had gone too far in attempting to exclude Yeltsin. At the next morning's session, Aleksei I. Kazannik, a law professor from Siberia, declared that he would forfeit his place in the Supreme Soviet if the Congress would agree to give the seat to Boris Yeltsin instead. Without a word of dissent, Yeltsin was then named to replace Kazannik in the Supreme Soviet.

That afternoon, as the Congress of People's Deputies completed its work for the day, a joyous crowd gathered in front of the Palace of Congresses to celebrate Yeltsin's victory. And as their hero left the hall and turned the corner to walk home to his apartment on Gorky Street, hundreds of men, women, and children marched behind him, forming a grand victory parade through the streets of Moscow.

A meeting of the Congress of People's Deputies

On June 9, 1989, the Congress of People's Deputies concluded its 13 days of meetings. As chairman of the gathering, Gorbachev was to be the last to speak. He was well into his speech—about the historic nature of the Congress, the great

changes taking place in the Soviet land, and the overwhelming support of the people for the policies of *glasnost*,
perestroika, and democratization—when there was a commo-
tion at one of the microphones on the floor. One of the
delegates in the vast hall was demanding to be heard. Who
could that be now? Gorbachev may have thought as he looked
up from the podium.

It was Andrei Sakharov, asking for the floor one last time, to
respond to something the general secretary had said.
Throughout the proceedings of the Congress, Sakharov had
been Gorbachev's most vocal critic. Silenced in Gorky for all
those years, now he would not waste a single opportunity to let
his voice be heard.

Gorbachev realized that if he was ever to gain the complete
trust of those who respected Sakharov, he must not be seen as
trying to silence the great scientist. Throughout the proceedings
of the Congress, therefore, Gorbachev had granted Sakharov
the floor whenever he rose to speak. But now, here was
Sakharov once again, interrupting the general secretary's con-
cluding remarks. Gorbachev sighed. Sakharov could have five
more minutes, he said, to make his points.

The Congress was not the great victory Gorbachev claimed,
Sakharov said. Though it marked a step toward democracy,
there had been no real transfer of power from the party to the
democratically elected representatives of the people. For there
to be true democracy in the Soviet Union, Sakharov continued,
the leading role of the Communist Party in Soviet society must
be ended. With Gorbachev holding both the post of president
and that of general secretary, there was a dangerous concentra-
tion of power in the hands of one man, which had not occurred
since the days of Stalin, Sakharov pointed out. At that point,
just as Sakharov started to criticize the KGB, the general secretary announced that the speaker's time had run out. When
Sakharov pressed on, Gorbachev activated the time-limit buzzer
underneath the podium.

Sakharov could barely be heard over the buzzing signal, yet he continued to speak. All government officials had to be subject to recall by the Congress, Sakharov argued.

"Please respect the Congress and be seated," Gorbachev pleaded.

"I respect humanity," the Nobel Prize winner responded. "I have a mandate that goes beyond the limit of this Congress."

"Then finish up," Gorbachev demanded.

"I am finishing," Sakharov answered. "I have left out a good deal." And then he went on speaking.

Finally, Gorbachev's patience was exhausted. "That's all!" he announced. "Your time allotment has run out."

Sakharov continued to speak. The Soviet ambassador to China, he said, must be recalled at once, in protest.

"That's all!" Gorbachev finally shouted. And with that he turned off the power to Sakharov's microphone.[3]

Gorbachev then declared that the Congress of People's Deputies was adjourned. The Supreme Soviet would begin its deliberations the next day. To conclude the session of the Congress, Gorbachev asked the assembled delegates to rise for the singing of the Soviet national anthem:

> *Unbreakable Union of free-born Republics,*
> *Great Russia has welded forever to stand;*
> *Created in struggle by will of the people,*
> *United and mighty, our Soviet Land!*
> *Sing to our Motherland, glory undying.*
> *Bulwark of peoples in brotherhood strong!*
> *Flag of the Soviets, people's flag flying,*
> *Lead us from victory to victory on!*

The delegates still sang as one, Gorbachev may have thought as he stood alone at the front of the hall. But he may also have noticed that there was less confidence in their voices than when they had sung the same song at congresses in the past.

chapter 4

Beijing: Tragedy at Tiananmen

The specially equipped Ilyushin-62 jetliner touched down gently on the runway of Beijing's Capital Airport. As the pilot brought the airplane to a stop at the edge of the tarmac, he noticed perhaps a dozen men dressed in business suits, most of them quite elderly, and a couple of women wearing brightly colored dresses hurrying to take their places about 20 feet from the foot of the carpeted stairway that was now being attached to the aircraft. Just beyond them a simple wooden stage had been set up. Its flimsy appearance suggested that it had been built only a short time before the plane's arrival.

This was all very curious, the pilot thought. Apparently there was going to be some kind of ceremony right here at the airport. The last he had been told when they had left Moscow was that there was to be no airport reception. Instead his distinguished passenger, Mikhail Sergeyevich Gorbachev, general secretary of the Communist Party of the Soviet Union and chairman of the Supreme Soviet, was to be taken directly by limousine to the center of Beijing where he was to exchange greetings with leaders of the Chinese Communist Party and government in a ceremony at Tiananmen Square. But judging from the speakers' platform and the small crowd gathered at the airport, there had apparently been a change in plans.

In fact, the Chinese authorities had been forced to change the site of the welcoming ceremony for Gorbachev because they were

Soviet leader Mikhail Gorbachev (*center*) and Chinese president
Yang Shangkung review troops at Beijing's Capital Airport just after
Gorbachev's arrival in China.

no longer in control of Tiananmen Square. On the day of
Gorbachev's arrival in Beijing—May 15, 1989—the square was
occupied by some 150,000 students demanding political reform
and democracy. Although the students in the square would
probably have provided Gorbachev with a much warmer reception than the rather stiff and polite ceremony organized by the
Chinese leadership at Capital Airport, government authorities
would not even consider allowing the students to greet the Soviet
hero. Many of the students looked upon Gorbachev as a
leader—more creative and energetic than the frail, conservative
old men who ruled their own country. Indeed, scattered among
the students' banners demanding human rights and political

freedom for the Chinese people were pictures of Mikhail Gorbachev. The students' chants of slogans in favor of political reform and a less restrictive society were now at times punctuated with cries of "Gorby! Gorby!" and "Perestroika!"

The Chinese leadership was very angry that the student demonstrations had erupted now of all times—at the start of the first visit of a Soviet leader to China since 1959. For almost 30 years, China and the USSR, the world's two largest Communist states, had been involved in a bitter dispute. In 1956 the Chinese Communist leadership headed by Mao Zedong had reacted with alarm when the Soviet leader Nikita Khrushchev spoke out against the crimes of the late Soviet dictator, Josef Stalin. When Khrushchev stepped up his accusations against Stalin and began to take tentative steps to reform Soviet society, the Chinese Communists accused him of "revisionism"—that is, of turning his back on the "true" teachings of Marxism-Leninism. Khrushchev reacted angrily, calling the Chinese "dogmatists" who cared more about holding onto political power for themselves than they did about truly serving the cause of the world's working classes.

For almost 30 years, the Soviet and Chinese leaders had been hurling these kinds of insults at each other. The two countries' political differences also served to irritate a long-standing border dispute between them. Over the past few decades, there had been several armed clashes in central Asia along the 4,000-mile boundary between the USSR and China.

But now Mao Zedong had been dead for 13 years, and Gorbachev represented a new generation of leaders in the Kremlin. And though the elderly Chinese leadership remained skeptical about Gorbachev's talk of "reforming" Communism, questions of doctrine and control of the world Communist movement now seemed less important than they had in the past. Both sides were more concerned with enjoying the gains resulting from cooperation in commerce and trade. Gorbachev's visit to Beijing in May 1989 would mark the start of a new era in relations between the two largest Communist states.

But now, it seemed, the student demonstrators in Tiananmen Square were stealing the world's attention from what was supposed to be a great celebration of renewed cooperation between China and the Soviet Union. Shielding Gorbachev from the hundreds of thousands of students gathered in the heart of Beijing would not be easy for the Chinese authorities. Not only had the government been forced to hold the ceremony welcoming Gorbachev to China at the airport, but now it had to change its plans for transporting the Soviet leader to the capital. Demonstrators were blocking the route by which Gorbachev was to be taken to his guest house. Instead of driving into the capital along a broad, modern avenue decorated with Chinese and Soviet flags, Gorbachev had to be transported along a series of narrow, congested, inconvenient back roads on the outskirts of the city—a route that took more than twice as long as originally planned.

Other plans also had to be changed. Gorbachev was supposed to lay a wreath at the monument to the Chinese revolution at the center of Tiananmen Square. But because of the students crowding the square, the wreath-laying ceremony was canceled. His meeting later in the day with the Chinese head of state, Yang Shangkung, was delayed two hours so that Gorbachev's route into the city could be cleared of demonstrators. Then the Soviet leader was to meet President Yang at the front door of Beijing's Great Hall of the People. When the crowds from Tiananmen Square drew too near the front entrance of the hall, word was relayed that Gorbachev was to use the Great Hall's side entrance instead. A few minutes later, another change in plans had to be made. There were now vast crowds at the side entrance as well. The Soviet leader was to be driven from his guest house—in an unmarked car, not the customary state limousine—to the rear entrance of the Great Hall of the People, the service entrance generally used by those coming to make repairs or deliver supplies. Exasperated by all the changes being made in his schedule, and exhausted by his hosts' efforts to "protect" him, Gorbachev finally turned to the Soviet ambassador to China and exclaimed, "Who the hell is in charge here?"[1]

▼ ▲ ▼

The unrest that filled the streets of China during the spring of 1989 had not begun with the arrival of Mikhail Gorbachev in Beijing on May 15. Nor did it come to an end when the Soviet leader left China three days later.

The roots of the people's discontent went back several years. Mao Zedong's death in 1976 had set off an intense power struggle within the Chinese Communist Party. On one side was a radical Communist faction led by Mao's wife, Jiang Qing, and three of her associates. This group, which later became known as the Gang of Four, insisted that China must remain true to the uncompromising brand of Communism favored by Mao. On the other side was a more moderate faction within the party that believed that modernizing the country's economy and increasing foreign trade were more important to China's future than defending "pure" Communist ideals at all costs.

Eventually the moderates managed to seize control of the Communist Party from the Gang of Four. One of Mao's chief rivals within the party, Deng Xiaoping, soon became the most powerful man in China. Quickly, Deng and his supporters instituted a program of far-reaching reforms to modernize China's economy. Peasants were given land, which they were allowed to farm as they wished. They were also permitted to sell what they produced at open markets. Private shops and restaurants in the cities could now compete with those owned by the government. Foreign corporations were encouraged to invest heavily in Chinese enterprises, and Chinese markets were opened to a wide array of foreign-made consumer goods. Once, when critics within China charged that the new policies seemed more like capitalism than socialism, Deng responded, "It doesn't matter if a cat is black or white; it only matters if it can catch mice."[2] To Deng and his followers, it no longer mattered whether China's system was purely socialist or whether it also had characteristics of capitalism. More important was whether the system led to a more prosperous and comfortable life for China's 1 billion people.

In spite of their willingness to introduce broad changes in their country's economy, however, Deng and his supporters refused to consider making major changes in China's political system. The word of the Communist Party still was law. No opposition political groups were allowed, and there were no free elections. The news media were still under government control

A Chinese man stands in front of a television display in a department store. The reforms instituted by Deng Xiaoping and his supporters helped modernize the Chinese economy and led to a more prosperous and comfortable life for the Chinese.

and heavily censored, and public criticism of government policies was strictly forbidden.

Increasingly, however, many Chinese came to believe that
China's economy could never be truly free as long as people
were controlled by the Communist Party. By the end of 1986,
students and professors at some of China's leading universities
began holding public demonstrations, seeking greater freedom.
In December of 1986, thousands of students marched through
the center of Beijing demanding democracy.

The protesting students soon discovered that they had a powerful supporter at the highest level of the Chinese Communist
Party. General Secretary Hu Yaobang refused to move against
the protesters, insisting instead that the students be allowed to
express their views openly. Hu went even further and
announced that he agreed with many of the students' demands!
If there was no political reform within China, Hu insisted, then
the country's economic reforms would eventually come to a halt.

China's other Communist leaders, however, including Hu's
close friend Deng Xiaoping, did not think the general secretary's
outspokenness was appropriate. At a meeting of the Communist
Party's Politburo in January 1987, Hu was replaced as general
secretary by Zhao Ziyang. The Politburo issued a statement
blaming Hu for "mistakes on major issues of political principles," including taking the side of the protesting students.[3]

While some leaders within the party—including Hu's replace-
ment as general secretary, Zhao Ziyang—still favored making a
few cautious reforms, most of China's other leaders continued to
resist change. Following Hu's dismissal as party leader, they
moved to silence all whose views differed from their own. Fang
Lizhi, one of China's most vocal defenders of human rights, was
fired from his post as vice president of Hefei University and was
also removed from membership in the Communist Party. Then
conservative Communists stepped up their criticism of Hu
Yaobang and demanded that he be thrown out of the Communist
Party. The strain finally became too much for Hu. He suffered a

heart attack at a meeting of the Politburo early in April 1989. A week later, he died at a Beijing hospital.

Many of Beijing's students were saddened and angered by the death of the man who had spoken out for them. On the morning of April 18, men and women in China's capital awoke to read the students' deepest feelings scrawled on banners hanging from their university's main buildings. One banner read, "Xiaoping is still healthy at age 84; Yaobang, only 73 years old, has died first." Another banner asked, "When you lost your post, why didn't we stand up? We feel guilty. Our conscience bleeds."[4]

Within hours, several thousand students from schools all over the capital gathered at Beijing University and then headed toward the center of the city. They were marching, they said, in memory of Hu Yaobang. As they marched, they sang songs of the Chinese revolution and shouted slogans in favor of democracy. And though they were turned away by police long before they reached the city's center, the students realized that on that day, a new prodemocracy movement had been launched in China.

The government was alarmed and quickly issued a ban on all public protests. Students taking part in illegal gatherings would be immediately expelled from their colleges. Demonstrators who refused to disperse would be arrested and prosecuted.

The students ignored the decrees of the government. By April 22, nearly 200,000 people had gathered in Tiananmen Square to demand greater political freedom. When the police attempted to seal off the square, tens of thousands of students held their ground and refused to leave. Their leaders announced that instead of returning to their homes they would camp overnight in the square. Groups of students would remain camped in Tiananmen Square, in the very center of the Chinese capital, for the next six weeks.

As their numbers grew larger, the students also became more organized. A 21-year-old freshman from Beijing University,

A student wades through a pile of memorial wreaths to Communist leader Hu Yaobang.

Wuer Kaixi, was named chairman of the organizing committee formed to represent students from the capital's various universities. Wang Dan, a 20-year-old history major at the same school, was chosen as chief spokesperson for the group. Among the first statements issued by the students was a simple proposal: If the government agreed to enter into formal talks with representatives of the organizing committee, then the students would end their demonstrations and leave Tiananmen Square. The students' proposal was immediately rejected by the Chinese government.

The next day a huge crowd of students marched from Beijing University toward Tiananmen. All along the 10-mile route into the city, thousands joined the students. Hundreds of thousands of other citizens stood at the side of the road, applauding heartily as the students passed by. A squadron of troops called in to halt the march was forced to fall back, completely outnumbered by the students, who forged ahead toward the square.

By the beginning of May, similar though smaller demonstrations in favor of political reform were being staged in other Chinese cities, including Shanghai, Changsha, Nanjing, Wuhan, and Xian. In Beijing, meanwhile, 3,000 students announced that they would go on a hunger strike until their demands were met. Within the Communist Party, the divide separating the moderates and the hard-liners was widening. At a very tense meeting of the Politburo on May 14, the party leaders agreed to allow Zhao Ziyang to open negotiations with the students—at least while Mikhail Gorbachev was visiting China.

Gorbachev's visit served only to encourage and embolden the striking students further. Now they added another demand to their proposals for political reform: the removal of Deng Xiaoping and Premier Li Peng.

▼ ▲ ▼

On May 18, Zhao was shown on national television visiting with several students who had been hospitalized as a result of their participation in the hunger strike. The general secretary looked concerned and worried. Later the same day the government accepted one of the students' demands: a meeting between Zhao and Premier Li and representatives of the students' organizing committee would be broadcast live on national television. At the meeting inside Beijing's Great Hall of the People, the student leaders boldly stated their case. Wuer Kaixi even criticized the premier for arriving at the meeting late! But while Zhao Ziyang continued to seek reconciliation with the students, Li Peng was as unbending as ever, seemingly unconcerned that he had become perhaps the most unpopular man in the entire country. He did not mince words with the students gathered before him. The chaos in Beijing was spreading to other parts of the country, Li Peng warned, and his government would never negotiate with hooligans and criminals who wanted to force China off the road to socialism. It was time for the students to return to their classes, Li said in conclusion, before the patience of the authorities was completely exhausted.[5]

Very early the next morning, Premier Li Peng agreed to accompany his rival, Zhao Ziyang, to Tiananmen. The Politburo had decided to give Zhao one more chance to persuade the students to leave the square. In tears, his voice thick with emotion, Zhao told the students, "We have come too late, too late." He then said, "You have good intentions. You want our country to become better. The problems you have raised will eventually be solved."[6] But matters were complicated, Zhao added, and the students must end their hunger strike and work with the government in resolving the country's crisis.

In spite of Zhao's pleas, the strike continued, and the crowd in Tiananmen Square continued to grow. Many believed that there were now as many as 1 million demonstrators in the streets of Beijing. With the blessing of Deng Xiaoping, Li Peng and the other hard-liners within the Chinese Communist Party now prepared to make their move.

Shortly after midnight on Saturday, May 20, Premier Li Peng appeared on national television. "We must adopt firm and resolute measures to end the turmoil swiftly," the prime minister said. "If we fail to put an end to such chaos immediately and let it go unchecked, it will very likely lead to a situation which none of us want to see."[7]

Martial law was declared in parts of Beijing, and citizens were forbidden from traveling into the center of the city. Foreign journalists were banned from interviewing people on the streets, and the government ordered the Cable News Network to halt live transmissions from Tiananmen Square. When CNN continued its broadcasts, Communist authorities turned off the power in CNN's Beijing studio, right in the middle of a transmission.

In spite of reports that thousands of troops were now being assembled on the outskirts of the capital, hundreds of thousands of Chinese students continued to defy their government's orders to leave the square. It was almost as though an independent, self-governing city had been established at the very center of the Chinese capital. The students now had an information center that issued frequent news bulletins to representatives of the world press. There was also a small hospital where the sick and injured could be treated, as well as a pharmacy that dispensed both Western-style medical prescriptions and traditional Chinese herbal remedies. There was a central dining hall where the students could come to eat, and a kitchen where the donations of food that kept arriving from people all across Beijing could be prepared. The students even had their own bank, where they were able to cash checks and take out small loans.

But life in the square was not easy. Some who spent the night there were able to find an unoccupied sleeping mat inside a tent, but many more had to spend the night outside on the cold pavement of the square. There was no running water, and only a few makeshift showers. Beijing authorities had cut off the square's access to the city's sewage and garbage collection systems. In spite of the help received from people around the city, most meals generally consisted of a few pieces of bread, a little rice, and some kind of hot or cold beverage.

In the very heart of the square, directly facing the large portrait of Chairman Mao Zedong that hung from the Gate of Heavenly Peace, the students had erected a 27-foot-high plaster and plastic-foam statue that was to serve as the symbol of their protest. The statue, a woman holding a torch aloft, was likened by many foreign observers to the Statue of Liberty in New York Harbor. The students named their statue the Goddess of Freedom.

For more than a week after Li Peng's declaration of martial law, China's authorities made feeble efforts to move troops into the capital to clear the students from the square. Day after day, long lines of military trucks armed with tear gas launchers or water cannons would drive several miles into the city, only to be

The Goddess of Freedom, erected by students in Tiananmen Square, was a symbol of their protest.

met by hundreds of men, women, and children. These "human roadblocks" would surround the military vehicles while others tried to convince the drivers to turn back. At first, the human roadblocks were successful. Many of the troops who were ordered into Beijing had come from remote provinces, far from the capital. Their officers had told them that they were being sent to rescue the government from a "counterrevolutionary rebellion" that threatened to topple the People's Republic and restore capitalism! The soldiers were genuinely shocked when they were informed that they were being sent to put down a group of unarmed students.

"We absolutely won't repress the people," one soldier told the crowd as he turned his truck around. "We are the people's soldiers." Another lieutenant broke into tears and sobbed, "I'll never come again. I'll never touch a hair on a student's head."[8] He then gave the order for his soldiers to return to their barracks. However, officials at the highest level of China's Communist Party were now convinced that they should use all means necessary to clear Tiananmen Square and crush the prodemocracy movement.

▼ ▲ ▼

On the morning of Saturday, June 3, tens of thousands of Beijing residents blocked Changan Boulevard, the main road into the city from the east and west, thus preventing thousands of heavily armed troops from marching into the square. Just to the west of the square, however, outside the headquarters of the Central Committee of the Chinese Communist Party, several hundred riot police used tear gas to break up the demonstrators. Angry students responded by throwing stones at the large plate-glass windows of the Great Hall of the People. There were reports that battalions of troops were now moving into the capital from all directions. Other rumors indicated that Beijing's central train station, which had been closed to the general public for several days, was now filled with soldiers from all over the country. Apparently the government had had such difficulty moving troops into the capital by road that they were using trains instead. Still others reported that they had heard that the government had used underground tunnels and now had thousands of soldiers stationed inside the Great Hall itself, on the very edge of Tiananmen Square.

As night came, a tense calm fell upon Tiananmen. Many believed that the government might move against the students at any time. While 100,000 students had filled the square for a rock-and-roll concert the night before, now only 20,000 remained, occupying perhaps one quarter of the immense plaza. Occasionally a speaker would address the crowd through a megaphone. Few seemed to listen. A few sang songs or chatted quietly among themselves. Others napped. A special tent had been set up where students who wished to do so could write their last wills and testaments—just in case the troops came.

At around midnight, shots were heard on Fuxing Avenue, about five miles west of the square. There was a sound of shouting in the distance, then a great roar, which seemed to move closer with each passing minute. Then, all at once, the ground began to shake as armed personnel carriers turned the corner and moved toward the square. There was a loud crash, screaming voices, and all was confusion. By one o'clock in the morning of Sunday, June 4, thousands of heavily armed troops swarmed into Tiananmen Square from all directions. Sharpshooters appeared atop the wall of the Great Hall of the People, then all along the top of the large tomb where the embalmed body of Mao lay in state. A row of soldiers fired tear gas canisters directly into the crowd of students. When the students refused to move, the soldiers surged forward, automatic rifles in their hands. When the students still refused to budge, the police used their rifles as clubs and beat the young people fiercely. If, even then, some students still held their places, they were shot dead at point-blank range.

Then the heavy artillery arrived. Heavily armed tanks streamed down Changan Boulevard—the Boulevard of Eternal Peace—followed by armed personnel carriers, on top of which were helmeted soldiers manning huge submachine guns. The Chinese People's Army was on the move—against the Chinese people.

There was a loud crash as the tanks broke through the barricades at the side of the square. When groups of protesters tried to form human roadblocks to stop the advancing artillery, the tanks just rolled on, crushing the students beneath their heavy treads. Armed vehicles poured into the square, flattening the students' tents as they went. There was another loud crash as the Goddess of Freedom hurtled to the ground, shattering into thousands of pieces as it fell.

At six o'clock on the morning of June 4, the heavy artillery of the Chinese Twenty-Seventh Army launched its last assault. When the square was finally completely cleared, more troops marched in, throwing all evidence of the massacre that had occurred into large bonfires. Morning news broadcasts on Chinese television congratulated the People's Liberation Army for successfully crushing a "counterrevolutionary rebellion" in the capital. According to a Chinese government spokesperson, 300 "troops, thugs, and spectators" had been killed in the violence around Tiananmen Square. In addition, government sources said, 5,000 troops had been wounded. Students had also destroyed 31 government trucks, 23 police cars, 2 armored personnel carriers, and 31 buses. The number of injured civilians was placed at around 2,000.[9]

Gradually, however, the world learned the truth about the horrible tragedy that had occurred. Most sources indicated that as many as 5,000 people may have been killed as a result of the army's actions in and around Beijing. In addition, a steady stream of the wounded filled the capital's hospitals for several days. There were reports of scores of patients dying when the city's blood supply ran out. Some doctors were said to have had to stay at their posts caring for the injured 72 consecutive hours.

Voices the world over joined in condemning the Chinese gov-

A man stands passively in front of a convoy of tanks.

ernment's actions. But Deng Xiaoping and Li Peng turned a deaf ear to world public opinion. Instead they moved as quickly as they could to get rid of what remained of the prodemocracy movement in other large Chinese cities.

Within a few days of the bloody massacre of June 4, traffic along the Boulevard of Eternal Peace had returned to normal. It took the Twenty-Seventh Army several more days to gain control of Beijing's various neighborhoods. Citizens armed only with sticks and stones continued to try to stop the advancing troops. The day following the great massacre in the square, a single student stood before a line of tanks as they rolled down Changan Boulevard. The tanks came to a halt when the student refused to move. Only when his friends pulled him away did the convoy of tanks continue its journey to the square. The young man had failed in his mission to stop the tanks' advance, but to millions of people around the world, his brave stand became a symbol of the heroism of the students in Tiananmen Square and of the hope of all those in China who still yearned for freedom.

chapter 5

Budapest: Heroes Remembered

On June 16, 1989, six coffins were laid to rest in a cemetery on the outskirts of Budapest, Hungary. Five of the coffins contained the remains of men who had been dead for 31 years. The sixth was empty.

The area seemed more like a beautifully landscaped park than a cemetery. Fresh grass seed had been scattered just a few weeks before, and now the tender blades were emerging at last from the ground. Young trees that had just been planted still seemed small and weak. They were bare now except for a few small, delicate leaves that had begun to sprout from their branches. But everyone knew that they would grow into tall, strong trees as the years went by. In future springs, they would grace the burial plot with elegant blossoms and foliage, and the air would also be sweetened with the fragrance of roses, lilacs, and jasmine.

Wide, well-paved walkways led up a gentle hill where six fresh graves had been dug. To each side, a soldier atop a pedestal stood at attention. A few feet away stood row after row of small wooden grave markers, carved in the traditional Hungarian manner. There were 260 markers in all, one for each of the 260 heroes who had died more than 30 years before.

The devoted Communist Matyas Rakosi had ruled the Communist Hungarian People's Republic since its establishment in 1948. However, when Stalin died in 1953, the new, somewhat more liberal Soviet leader, Nikita Khrushchev, ordered Rakosi to turn over control of the Hungarian government to his chief rival, a reform-minded Communist named Imre Nagy. Rakosi was allowed to retain his position as leader of Hungary's Communist Party.

Imre Nagy was a lifelong, dedicated Communist, who had spent many years in training in the Soviet Union. However, he had grown increasingly sickened and angered by the brutality of the Stalinist system and believed that he could establish a more democratic form of socialism within his country. In July 1953, Nagy presented his proposals for a "New Course" for Hungary to the country's parliament. However, the reformist government of Imre Nagy did not have the support of the Stalinist Communist Party of Matyas Rakosi, and the split between the two continued to widen. Early in 1954, Khrushchev changed his mind and gave in to Rakosi's demands that Nagy be removed from office.

People throughout Hungary were bitterly disappointed by this turn of events. Nagy had become perhaps the most popular man in the country, and many Hungarians had grown so fond of their new prime minister that they had taken to calling him Uncle Imre. In the summer of 1956, Khrushchev received word of a plot by Rakosi to have Nagy and 400 of his supporters arrested, perhaps even executed. When the Soviet leader realized that he had made a mistake in siding with the old Stalinist rather than with the reformer Nagy, he ordered Rakosi to come to Moscow for "medical treatment." Rakosi would remain in the Soviet Union until his death in 1971.

Most Hungarians were elated when they heard the news that Khrushchev had fired Rakosi. However, when they learned that Rakosi's closest advisor, Ernö Gerö, was to become the new head of the Hungarian party, they were very disappointed. Gerö had carried out many of the former dictator's most unpopular orders. "In place of a bald Rakosi, we now have a thin one!" many remarked sadly.[1] Now, Hungarians wanted genuine change.

In October 1956, Hungarian university students began meeting to discuss the need for political reform in their country. On October 23, over 100,000 people gathered in Republic Square in Budapest to press their demands for human rights, political democracy, an end to Soviet interference in their country's affairs, and the restoration of the government of Imre Nagy.

The same day a few blocks west of Republic Square, another crowd gathered outside of Budapest's central radio station. Several teenagers were trying to batter down the wooden gate of the wall that surrounded the station. Time and again, they backed an old automobile against the gate. Each time the wooden door creaked and seemed to weaken, yet held against the teenagers' efforts. Others in the crowd threw stones and bricks against the wide windows on the station's first floor, demanding to be let in. Finally the security policemen gathered inside the station had had enough. A canister of tear gas was fired into the crowd. Horrified, the crowd watched as the canister hit the face of a teenage boy and then exploded, killing him instantly and disfiguring his body terribly.

Then, all at once, more shots rang out. Several other students fell to the ground, mortally wounded. Now the crowd became enflamed, and soon hundreds of people were battering against the radio station's entrance. Finally the old door fell, and the crowd rushed in—right into the line of fire of a squad of security police, who had been lying in wait for hours.

Quickly the government moved more troops into the center of Budapest. Soldiers began to fire at random into the crowds. But instead of fleeing, the people pressed in closer. Fighting soon spread to Stalin Square just to the north, where thousands had gathered with a single goal in mind: destruction of the massive 50-foot bronze statue of the hated Soviet dictator Stalin. It took the crowd several hours, but with the aid of blowtorches aimed at the statue's ankles and steel cables tied around its neck, the statue eventually came toppling to the ground. As the crowd cheered, the once-mighty monument broke into pieces. The head, however, remained largely intact, and on Stalin's brow

In Budapest, Hungary, a crowd gathers around the toppled statue of
Joseph Stalin.

one teenager fastened a road sign that read, "Dead End."

In the aftermath of these events, Gerö decided to invite Imre
Nagy to form a new government. While he had no intention of
granting Nagy real power, he hoped that the presence of "Uncle
Imre" would be enough to bring the rebellion to a halt. At the
same time, Gerö sent an urgent plea to Moscow, asking for more

Soviet troops to help him put down the "counterrevolution" that now threatened Communist Hungary. When Nagy arrived at his office, Gerö immediately ordered him placed under house arrest. A squad of security police was ordered to guard the new prime minister around the clock. Early the next morning, Gerö handed Nagy a script to be read over the national radio. The new prime minister was to tell the people of Hungary that a state of emergency had been proclaimed and that all those fighting the government should immediately lay down their arms. Gerö commanded that Nagy read the speech as written. Not a single word was to be changed. To make sure that he obeyed, Gerö ordered two security officers, pistols drawn, to stand just behind Nagy as he read the statement over the air.

But the rebellion still spread. A long line of cars, trucks, and bicycles streamed toward Budapest. People from villages across Hungary were now heading for the capital "to save Uncle Imre" and help bring down the Communist state. They brought weapons with them to help arm the "Freedom Fighters." On the second day of the rebellion, the capital's entire police force switched sides and joined the battle against the Communists. There were also reports that units of the Hungarian army were defecting and joining the side of the rebellion as well.

On October 24, Khrushchev removed Gerö from office. Soviet representatives in Budapest then informed Nagy that he was free to act as prime minister—but only on the condition that he move forcibly against the "counterrevolution." Sickened by the thought of unleashing further violence on his own people, Nagy begged the Soviet leaders for one more chance to negotiate a settlement.

Three days later, Prime Minister Nagy announced the formation of a new coalition government, which was to include several prominent non-Communists. The next day, the Soviet government announced that it would begin immediately to withdraw its troops from Hungary. Within hours, people were dancing, rather than battling, in the streets of Budapest. They believed they had won a great victory over the retreating Soviet army.

▼ ▲ ▼

Beyond Budapest, however, the fighting continued. Many
Hungarians in the countryside ignored Nagy's pleas to put
down their weapons. Instead they pledged to battle on to overthrow all traces of Hungarian Communism. Even when Nagy
named several prominent non-Communists to yet another reor-
ganized government—and even announced the end of
Hungary's one-party system and promised free elections in the
future—the anti-Communist forces pressed for further conces-
sions. They demanded that all Soviet troops be withdrawn from
Hungary immediately and that Hungary withdraw from the
Warsaw Pact.

On October 31, Nagy received reports that the Soviet Union
had halted the withdrawal of its troops and was now massing soldiers at its borders with Hungary in preparation for an even
larger invasion. Feeling betrayed by the Soviets, Nagy summoned their ambassador, Yuri Andropov, to this office and
informed him that Hungary was withdrawing from the Warsaw
Pact and would no longer be bound to the Soviet Union.

Andropov immediately informed his superiors in Moscow that
Nagy had lost control of the country and that Hungary's future
as a socialist state was threatened. Throughout the next day,
preparations for a large-scale invasion of the country were
made. On November 2, the Soviet foreign ministry announced
that Hungary was in the grips of an "antisocialist counterrevolution," and that Nagy himself was the leading traitor.

On November 4, thousands of Soviet troops stormed into
Budapest, crushing all efforts to resist on the part of the
Hungarians. Within hours, Nagy and his government were sur-
rounded in the parliament building. All telephone and telegraph
lines were cut, and with them Hungary's connections with the
outside world. The new leader of the Hungarian Communist Party,
Janos Kadar, proclaimed the formation of a new "Hungarian
Government of Revolutionary Workers and Peasants." Kadar also

announced that his government was "requesting" the assistance of the Soviet army in restoring "law and order" to the country.

For another week, fierce fighting raged in the streets of Budapest. By the time the Soviet takeover of the city was completed, 3,000 had been killed, 13,000 wounded, and over 4,000 buildings had been destroyed. In addition, some 200,000 Hungarians had seized the opportunity to escape across the border into Austria.

When he saw that all was lost, Imre Nagy sought protection from the Soviets in the Yugoslav embassy. After spending two weeks there, he finally accepted offers from Janos Kadar to leave the embassy and enter into "negotiations" about the future of the country. The Soviet ambassador Andropov also promised that Nagy would not be harmed if he left the embassy.

Nagy walked out of the embassy grounds and boarded a bus that, he thought, was to take him to his home on the outskirts of Budapest. Instead, just as the bus began to drive off, two Soviet secret police agents jumped aboard as well. Nagy was taken to the airport and flown to Romania for "safe keeping."

Kadar's new government quickly launched a campaign against "counterrevolutionaries." Over 20,000 Hungarians were sent to prison, and thousands of others were deported to labor camps in the USSR. Special laws were passed to speed up the prosecution of "traitors." Under these revised laws, 2,000 additional Freedom Fighters were executed for their roles in the October uprising. If a convicted counterrevolutionary was under age, the new law allowed his execution to be delayed until the day the defendant turned 18. Kadar was determined that not a single traitor go unpunished.

In early June of 1958, Imre Nagy was brought back to Hungary in chains and secretly placed on trial for leading the 1956 counterrevolution. On June 16, an announcement on Radio Budapest informed the world that Nagy and his closest advisors had been executed for treason. The Communists secretly buried the bodies of the executed men in an isolated part of the public cemetery just beyond the prison where they had been shot. This area, known as Plot 301, was also the final resting place of 260 others executed for their roles in the Budapest uprising. There their bodies lay, neglected and forgotten, for the better part of three decades. In time, Plot 301 became overgrown with weeds and brush. Soon it was even being used as a dumping ground and was littered with trash and garbage.

But the Hungarian people remembered the story of 1956. And, in time they learned of the location of Nagy's body. The friends and families of the heroes of 1956 waited and hoped for the time for justice to come at last.

▼ ▲ ▼

As soon as Janos Kadar had crushed the Budapest uprising, he moved at once to put the events of 1956 behind him. "He who is not against us is with us," Kadar declared.[2] As long as reformers did not attack the basic Communist principles of the country or call into question Hungary's unwavering loyalty to the Soviet Union, they would not be bothered by his "centrist" Communist government, insisted Kadar.

Kadar also saw the need to improve the living standards of Hungary's people. In 1968, his government introduced the New Economic Mechanism (N.E.M.), which allowed local managers of factories and farms considerable freedom in fixing prices and determining wages. A program of profit sharing was established that encouraged more productive labor. Hungarian market-places soon boasted a wider assortment of goods and services than were available in other Eastern European countries.

Still, "Kadarism" failed in its attempts to bring the Hungarian economy up to the levels of its capitalist neighbors, Austria and West Germany. When the cost of imported oil rose dramatically during the 1970s, the Hungarian economy struggled to keep up. Increased trade with Western nations led to a huge foreign debt. Unemployment and inflation became problems in Hungary for the first time since the end of World War II.

The rise of Mikhail Gorbachev in the Soviet Union in the 1980s led many Hungarians to yearn for political reform as well. The pressure to "follow Gorbachev" became so great that in May 1988, Janos Kadar was forced to turn over the leadership post he had held for over 30 years to a younger, reform-minded Communist named Karoly Grosz. Grosz bragged that Hungary was about to institute its own *perestroika*, under which the entire nation would be modernized and transformed.

As the first step in this political reform, the Communist government announced that the formation of independent political groups would be allowed for the first time since the Communist takeover. Grosz even hinted that multiparty elections might be possible at some point in the future. Seemingly overnight, hundreds of new political organizations emerged. Among the largest of these were the Hungarian Democratic Forum, the Alliance of Young Democrats, and the Network of Free Initiatives. Another group, the Committee for Historical Justice, was formed to keep alive the memory of Imre Nagy and his comrades. This group demanded that the Hungarian Supreme Court launch a full-scale investigation of the facts surrounding the 1956 rebellion and its aftermath.

The sudden rise of popular political rivals caught the Communists by surprise. In spite of the great show of unity that had greeted Grosz's appointment as party leader, a deep split was developing within the ruling Socialist Workers Party. One faction was led by radical reformers like Reszö Nyers and Imre Poszgay. This group saw Hungary gradually emerging as a free and open society with numerous political parties competing for power in democratic elections. Another faction, led by General Secretary Grosz and Gyula Thurmer, thought that reform had already gone too far and that the party should reassert its authority over Hungarian society and slow the pace of change.

At a party congress early in 1989, both sides agreed to an uneasy compromise. Grosz would now share leadership of the party with three well-known reformers: Nyers, Poszgay, and Miklos Nemeth. A few months later, following a long and heated debate, the party leadership voted to permit the public funeral and reburial of Imre Nagy. Further, the party decreed, the entire ceremony would be broadcast live on Hungarian state television! The government then moved to clean up the area around Plot 301 in Rakoskeresztur Cemetery. A stunning monument to those who had died was erected, and the Supreme Court agreed to investigate the events of 1956.

▼ ▲ ▼

On June 16, 1989, almost 200,000 people gathered in Heroes Square in Budapest. Six coffins stood on the steps of Budapest's Gallery of Art. Each was covered with a large bouquet of flowers and was surrounded by a circle of Hungarian flags. Each flag had a hole in its middle, like the flags carried by the Freedom Fighters of 1956, who had cut the Communist hammer-and-sickle emblem out of their flags when they waved them over Budapest more than 30 years before. Behind each coffin burned a large flame—a flame of hope, a flame of freedom. On five of the coffins a name was inscribed, with family name first, in the Hungarian manner: Losonczy, Geza—minister in the coalition government formed during the uprising; Maleter, Pal—defense minister in the same government; Szilagy, Jozsef—head of the prime minister's staff; Gimes, Miklos—the journalist who had alerted the world to the carnage taking place in Budapest. And, on the coffin on the top step: Nagy, Imre. The sixth coffin was reserved for the "Unknown Freedom Fighter." It would represent the thousands of unknown Hungarians who had given their lives for the cause of freedom on the streets of Budapest and in cities all across Hungary.

"Will freedom for Hungary grow from the blood of these heroes?" asked Sandor Racz, one of the speakers that day.[3] Racz was head of the Workers' Councils of Budapest during the uprising. He still remembered those events so long ago very clearly. Now, for the first time in 33 years, he could speak of them openly once again.

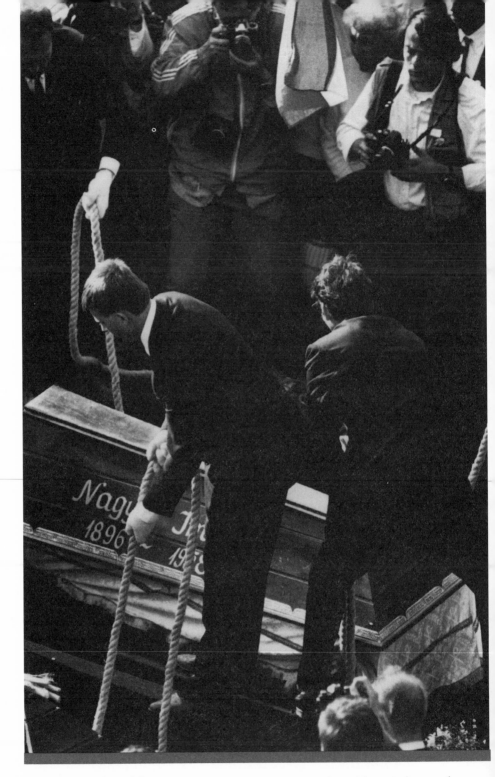

The coffin of former Hungarian prime minister Imre Nagy is lowered into the ground.

It is said that after his death sentence was pronounced, Imre Nagy rose from his seat in the Budapest courtroom and said, "If my life is needed to prove that not all Communists are enemies of the people, I gladly make the sacrifice. I know that one day there will be another Nagy trial, which will rehabilitate me. I also know that I will have a reburial. I only fear that the funeral oration will be delivered by those who betrayed me."[4]

But while several representatives of the Communist government were present in Budapest on the day Imre Nagy was reburied, including Prime Minister Miklos Nemeth and Minister of State Imre Poszgay, Janos Kadar did not attend the solemn ceremony. He remained at his villa outside of Budapest, a sick and broken man.

Less than one month later, on July 8, 1989, the Hungarian Supreme Court announced the results of its investigation into the events of 1956. Imre Nagy had been unjustly tried, unjustly sentenced, and unjustly executed, the court declared. He was not a traitor to the Hungarian nation, the court concluded, but rather a genuine hero.

That same day, Janos Kadar died in a Budapest hospital at the age of 77. It could be said that Communism in Hungary died with him, for throughout the summer of 1989, political events within Hungary began to move at a dizzying rate of speed. By the end of the year, the Communist system that had terrorized the country and claimed so many thousands of lives over its 40 years of existence would be a thing of the past.

Just days before the ceremony at Heroes Square, the Hungarian government had entered into negotiations with several of the leading opposition groups. As a result of these talks, an agreement was announced on September 18. The country's news media would no longer be censored, and opposition groups would be allowed their own newspapers and radio stations. All restrictions on the Catholic Church and other religious bodies would be lifted. The government also promised to protect freedom of speech and assembly. Finally, genuinely free elections, open to all parties, were scheduled for March 1990.

More than a dozen major opposition parties were formed. Before long, they were no longer only attacking their common enemy, the Communists, but were also clearly debating how they differed from one another. The nation's press now seemed completely uninterested in the official pronouncements of the Communist leaders. Instead, they wanted to know the views of Jozsef Antall, the leader of the Democratic Forum, on some issue. Or they wanted to print what Janos Kis of the Federation of Young Democrats had to say.

By now, too, the Communist party itself was in complete disarray. On October 7, a special congress of the party was convened in Budapest. It quickly became obvious that divisions had become too wide to bridge. On October 8, 1989, the Hungarian Socialist Workers Party voted itself out of existence! Many of the leading reform Communists, including Reszö Nyers and Imre Poszgay, joined together in a new Hungarian Socialist Party. Others, including Karoly Grosz and Gyula Thurmer, formed a more traditional Communist party that retained the name Hungarian Socialist Workers Party. Other party members eventually decided to join one of the new opposition parties instead of either Communist party.

Later in October Hungary's parliament met in Budapest. Despite the fact that the parliament was still officially controlled by the Communists, a new constitution was adopted that proclaimed the government was "an independent, democratic state based on the rule of law" in which the values of both multiparty democracy and democratic socialism would be equally recognized.[5] The constitutional clause declaring that the Communist Party had a "leading role" in Hungarian society was eliminated. Other changes were made to guarantee the independence of the court system and the police. Finally the parliament voted to change even the name of the country. The People's Republic of Hungary would no longer exist. From that moment forward the country would be simply the Republic of Hungary.

Thousands gathered in front of the parliament building on the banks of the Danube as the new republic was officially proclaimed. Church bells rang and the crowd cheered. Many of those present that day remarked on the appropriateness of the date. It was October 23. The Hungarian uprising had begun 33 years before, to the very day. Now, at last, the government had agreed to the demands made on that day.

Jozsef Antall, chairman of the Hungarian Democratic Forum

chapter 6

Berlin: The Wall Crumbles

Almost 50 miles long and more than 5 miles wide, Hungary's Lake Balaton ranks as the largest lake in Central Europe. For more than 100 years, it has been a popular vacation destination not only for Hungarians but also for people from neighboring lands. The establishment of Communist states in Hungary and East Germany (the German Democratic Republic, or GDR) following World War II served only to encourage the flow of German tourists to Balaton every summer. Although German citizens were generally forbidden even to visit relatives in democratic West Germany (the Federal Republic of Germany, or FRG), the Communist authorities in East Berlin had no qualms whatsoever about allowing East German citizens to travel south across Czechoslovakia into Hungary to take advantage of Balaton's well-developed and inexpensive tourist facilities.

However, the tide of political reform that swept over Hungary during the spring and summer of 1989 had a significant effect on relations between that country and East Germany. On May 2, 1989, the foreign ministry of the reform Communist government in Hungary announced that it was preparing to remove all fortifications along its western border with Austria. Within hours, Hungarian soldiers with wire cutters and pliers were dismantling the barbed wire fences along more than 100 miles of the once heavily guarded "iron curtain," as the barrier between Eastern and Western Europe was known.

Almost immediately many East Germans already vacationing in Hungary grasped the opportunity that lay before them. Scores of them made their way west from Lake Balaton to the foothills of the Alps along the Hungarian-Austrian border. Carefully avoiding the few troops who still patrolled the frontier, they streamed across the border into Austria and made their way to the West German embassy in the Austrian capital, Vienna.

As the time for summer vacations arrived, thousands of East Germans began secretly planning to escape to the West by way of Hungary. As in years gone by, they would board special tourist trains for Balaton or drive their small two-cylinder Trabant autos across Czechoslovakia and into Hungary. However, this summer, many had no intention of returning to East Germany when their vacations were over. Instead they too would head for Austria and freedom in the West.

In past years the Hungarian government had taken care to make sure that all foreign visitors returned to their homelands at the proper time. Now, however, the Hungarian Communists were too preoccupied with their own political survival—and too interested in reaching out to the democratic countries of Western Europe—to worry about helping the hard-line government of East Germany leader Erich Honecker exercise control over its people. Hungarian police no longer stopped East Germans as they poured into the West German embassy in Budapest. The Hungarian government even established several refugee camps to provide food and accommodations for East Germans who refused to return home. Thousands of Germans were now encamped across Hungary, patiently awaiting permission from the Hungarian authorities to leave for Austria or West Germany.

At the end of August, the Hungarian foreign minister Gyula Horn flew to East Berlin to consult with his East German counterpart, Oscar Fischer. Fischer demanded that Hungary carry out its 1969 agreement with the GDR to return forcibly any East Germans attempting to cross into Austria. Horn listened patiently to Fischer but then informed him that although the leaders of the Hungarian government wanted to maintain good relations with their fellow Communists in East Germany, they nevertheless now felt obligated to carry out the terms of the United Nations convention requiring the free passage of refugees. Thus, the Hungarian foreign minister concluded, Hungary had no choice but to suspend its agreement with the GDR and allow all East Germans who wished to cross into Austria.

On September 11, Hungary opened its border with Austria, allowing free passage to all who wanted to cross. By the end of the day, 20,000 East Germans had gone over to the West. Within a few weeks, they would be joined by more than 10,000 others who had spent the entire summer hiding in the homes of Hungarian friends, waiting for the right moment. The turn of events was amazing: A Communist government was actually assisting citizens of another Communist state to flee to the West!

Honecker's government in Berlin responded immediately by banning all travel by East Germans to Hungary. But those intent on gaining freedom would not be stopped. Unable to pass into Hungary, large crowds of East Germans began storming into the West German embassy in Prague, Czechoslovakia, demanding political asylum in the West. As thousands of would-be refugees crowded into the ill-equipped embassies, living conditions steadily worsened. Reluctantly, Honecker agreed to grant them permission to leave the country. But he attached a condition: The refugees would not be allowed to pass directly from Czechoslovakia into West Germany. Instead they would board trains that would be routed back into the GDR briefly. There, they would be stripped of their East German citizenship and then "expelled" to the Federal Republic. In this way, Honecker could at least claim that thousands of "undesirables" had been kicked out of East Germany.

However, Honecker's attempt to save face immediately back-fired. Rather than allowing thousands of emigrants to be transported quickly and quietly into West Germany from Czechoslovakia, he had created a public spectacle. As the three

On a train carrying them from East to West Germany, East Germans wave excitedly as they pass the border marker.

"freedom trains" pulled into the station in the East Germany city of Dresden, where the refugees were to be officially stripped of their citizenship, a crowd of several thousand bystanders rushed forward and attempted to jump on board. The police responded hastily and brutally, stopping all but a few from mounting the platform. The scene was repeated when the trains arrived at Karl Marx Stadt several hours later. When the trains finally crossed the border into the Federal Republic, the route was lined with thousands of West Germans, cheering, waving, and shouting words of encouragement to their fellow Germans.

By the end of the summer of 1989, almost 50,000 East Germans had left for the West. One observer estimated that over 2 million East Germans (out of the country's total population of 16.5 million) would move to West Germany if they had the chance. Among those who left—or who wanted to leave—were some of the most valuable members of East German society: doctors, teachers, scientists, technicians, and professionals who had grown weary of their bleak life under the Communist system. Disillusionment with the situation in East Germany had become so complete that one popular joke in the country during the summer of 1989 ended with the line "East Germany—would the last person out please turn off the lights?"

▼ ▲ ▼

Still, Erich Honecker persisted in making plans for a grand celebration to commemorate the fortieth anniversary of the founding of the Communist German Democratic Republic. There were to be parades and parties and political speeches. Soviet leader Mikhail Gorbachev had been invited as the guest of honor. He arrived in East Berlin on October 6, the day before the grand celebration was to take place.

As in Beijing earlier in the year, thousands gathered in the streets of East Berlin to hail Gorbachev as the great reformer of the socialist system. Banners quoting Honecker himself waved in the breeze. "To learn from the Soviet Union is to learn how to win!" the East German leader had proclaimed years before. Now, thousands of East Germans were demanding that their leaders truly follow the Soviet example and start a *perestroika*-like reform program in East Germany.

Soviet leader Mikhail Gorbachev in East Berlin

The next day, Honecker and Gorbachev appeared together, arms linked in friendship, at the celebration in East Berlin of the anniversary of the founding of the GDR. But beneath the surface, a deep difference of opinion now separated the two Communist leaders. Gorbachev had insisted in private talks with Honecker that the East Germany government embrace political reform. Under no circumstances, he said, would he allow Soviet troops to be sent to East Germany to defend Honecker's position. But the East German leader remained unmoved. Honecker had dedicated his life to the East German Communist system. In 1961, he had been the country's chief of security. Later he had supervised the construction of the Berlin Wall. As long as he was in power, Honecker told Gorbachev, East Germany would remain true to the ways of Marxism-Leninism, whether he was defended by the Soviets or not. In his speech before the East German people the next day, Gorbachev insisted openly that political systems needed to change with the times. When he force-fully warned, "Life itself punishes those who delay," few doubted that he had his East German hosts in mind.[1] At the conclusion of the anniversary festivities, Honecker accompanied his guest to the airport, and the two men embraced before Gorbachev boarded his plane for Moscow. As the Soviet leader went up the steps to his plane, the East German leader stood waving, all alone at the bottom of the stairs.

▼ ▲ ▼

Following Gorbachev's visit, demonstrations against the Honecker regime quickly spread throughout East Germany. On the evening of October 9, thousands marched in the southern city of Leipzig, under the leadership of a recently established reform group, New Forum. Every night for a week, demonstra-tions were held. Every night they were met by riot police with tear gas. But now the East German people did not seem to be frightened of the security police who had terrorized them for so long. Every night, the crowd seemed to grow a little larger. By October 16, it numbered more than 100,000 people—all demanding political reform, the right to travel freely, and an end to Honecker's rule.

Honecker declared that he would never negotiate with those who "trampled on the moral values of socialism." Furthermore, he said, there would be "no tears shed" over those who had chosen to flee to the West.[2] Then Honecker decided to put an end to the "counterrevolution," once and for all. On October 17, according to some reports, Honecker ordered the Leipzig police to arm them-selves with live ammunition and to open fire if need be to break up the demonstration planned for that evening. Horrified by the thought of the bloodbath that might take place, the GDR's chief of security, Egon Krenz, flew immediately to Leipzig. According to some sources, Krenz personally canceled Honecker's order. That night, over 120,000 peaceful demonstrators marched through the streets of the city unhampered by the police for the first time.

Now, even Honecker's own comrades were turning on their longtime leader. The next day, the Central Committee of the Communist Party forced Honecker to resign from office and named Egon Krenz to replace him as leader of the East German party, state, and armed forces. Krenz was the youngest member of the ruling Politburo. At the age of 51, he was a full 25 years younger than Honecker. Many Communists hoped that Krenz would be better able to respond quickly to the challenges the country now faced.

Immediately after assuming office, Krenz appeared on East German television, joking and smiling broadly—in sharp contrast to the stiff, formal manner of Honecker. "My motto remains work, work, work, and more work," he told his discontented fellow citizens, "but work that should be pleasant and serve all the people."[3]

Yet the people of East Germany were suspicious of the "new Krenz" who appeared before them. Few believed that a man who had worked his way up through the Communist Party as one of Honecker's most dedicated lieutenants could actually be any kind of "reformer." They remembered too clearly his years as chief of the Stasi, the East German ministry for state security, which controlled the much-hated secret police.

The tide of East Germans leaving for the West showed no signs of decreasing. Then, on November 4, the Communist government of Czechoslovakia announced that it too was opening its borders to all East Germans who wanted to cross into West Germany. Within hours, the line of East German autos at Schirnding on the Czech-German border stretched for more than 14 miles. Within a few days, 50,000 more East Germans had entered West Germany by way of Czechoslovakia.

Massive demonstrations—up to half a million people or more—soon filled the streets of East Berlin. All attempts by Krenz to reach a compromise were quickly rejected. Following the government's proposals for changes in the country's law on travel, for example, even more men and women took to the streets of the East German capital. Soon a new slogan was being chanted in cities across East Germany: "Egon Krenz, we're not your friends!" Others in the crowds would shout, "Egon raus!"—"Egon, get out!"

On November 7, the East German cabinet resigned, and Hans Modrow, a popular, reform-minded mayor of Dresden, was named as the new prime minister. But even the appointment of the man once lauded as "East Germany's Gorbachev" failed to quiet the protesters. Eventually a million East Berliners were demonstrating openly against their government.

Two days later, on November 9, Günter Schabowski, head of the GDR's ministry of press and information, held a news conference to report on a meeting of the Communist Party Politburo. Schabowski answered a few questions from reporters and then told them that he had one more statement to make. In a matter-of-fact voice, Schabowski announced that, starting immediately, citizens of the German Democratic Republic who desired to do so would be allowed to leave the country any time they wished. There would no longer be any need to slip out by way of Hungary, Austria, or Czechoslovakia. East Germans could pass to the Federal Republic directly through East German crossing points. All they needed was to obtain a permit, which would be granted at the borders to anyone who requested one.

All at once, it seemed, the East German Communist leaders had surrendered to the people. The Berlin Wall—the hated symbol of the Cold War between East and West—was now all but irrelevant. If East Germans could now travel freely to the West, if they could even leave the country for good if they desired, then what use was the wall, which separated East Berlin from West Berlin? For many East Germans, who had lived in the shadow of the hated Wall for almost 30 years, and who had lived under the oppression of the Communist system for more than 40 years, the news was like a dream come true.

That night the center of Berlin took on the atmosphere of a giant party, as East and West Berliners danced together atop the Wall. Some West German youths even climbed over to the other side to shake hands or present flowers to the East German border guards. The guards, who until the day before had been ordered to shoot to kill anyone who dared to approach the Wall, shook their heads in amazement at the wondrous turn of events.

The next day, the East German government declared a holiday, and hundreds of thousands of East Berliners streamed

East and West Berliners celebrate the fall of The Berlin Wall.

to the West. There were massive traffic jams as long lines of small East German Trabants slowly made their way under the Brandenburg Gate at the heart of the divided city, and through a newly created hole in the Wall. Subway lines connecting the two parts of the city were jammed for hours, and government officials announced that a shuttle bus service would be established to ease the congestion. Soon the East German government sent work crews to bulldoze five additional openings in the Wall that had once separated East from West.

Of the multitude of East Berliners who traveled west once the Wall was opened, relatively few decided to remain there permanently. The majority intended to return to their homes in the East later the same day. The first stop almost all made on the Western side was at a bank, where each East German could collect 100 deutsche marks (about $55 at the time) in "welcome money" offered by the government of the Federal Republic. Then many of the Eastern visitors would find their way to the fashionable Kurfurstendamm (or Ku-damm) shopping district in the center of West Berlin, where they would gaze longingly at the many beautiful but expensive goods for sale in the glamorous boutiques that lined the way. Almost everywhere they went, East Berliners were greeted warmly. One West Berliner offered free champagne to all who crossed. Restaurants gave out coupons for free meals. There were also offers of free movie tickets or guided tours of West Berlin. A popular Berlin soccer team even offered the visiting Easterners 10,000 free tickets to an upcoming match.

Now the East Germans could compare the two Germanys, and it was clear that living conditions in the West were far superior to those in the East. The Communists were completely discredited in the eyes of East Germans. Within six weeks of the opening of the Berlin Wall, Egon Krenz was forced out of office. He was replaced as party leader by Gregor Gysi, a young lawyer who had made a name for himself during the Honecker years by defending the civil rights of the government's most outspoken opponents. The Communist Party devised a new "revolutionary program," which declared, "The German Democratic Republic is in the midst of an awakening."[4] Genuinely free elections were planned for early 1990. Gysi expressed confidence that the elections would show that the people of East Germany did not want to turn their backs on socialism.

Most East Germans, however, had strikingly different ideas. With the collapse of the Berlin Wall, many people, both in the East and in the West, had begun to ask why Germany had to remain divided. More and more Germans wanted to know why Germany could not just become a united country once again.

chapter 7

Sofia: A Sleeping Nation Awakes

Following the defeat of Nazi Germany in World War II, the Bulgarian Communist Party under the leadership of Georgi Dimitrov emerged as the most powerful political force within Bulgaria. Thousands of the Communists' rivals for power were arrested, exiled, and even killed to prevent any challenge to the total Communist takeover of the country. That takeover was completed in December 1947 with the establishment of the People's Republic of Bulgaria.

Communist Bulgaria soon became the Soviet Union's most loyal ally. Dimitrov was a lifelong Communist who was completely dedicated to the policies of Stalin. In July 1949, however, Dimitrov died very suddenly while visiting Moscow. Most historians now believe that Stalin had Dimitrov poisoned, perhaps because he was jealous of the high esteem that Bulgarians had for their leader. A delegation from the Bulgarian government was sent to Moscow to bring the fallen leader's body back to the Bulgarian capital, Sofia. There, Dimitrov's preserved remains would lie in state under glass in a specially built mausoleum for almost 40 years.

In time a group of younger Communists within the party grew weary of the rule of the hard-line Stalinists who had followed Dimitrov. One member of this younger group was Todor Zhivkov, the leader of the Communist Party organization in Sofia. By 1956, Zhivkov had become the most powerful man within the Bulgarian Communist Party. He would hold tightly to his position for more than 30 years—nearly as long as the body of Dimitrov would lie undisturbed in its ornate tomb.

Like Dimitrov before him, Zhivkov tied his country as closely as possible to its Soviet protector. When the Soviet Union led Warsaw Pact troops in the invasion of Czechoslovakia in 1968, Zhivkov did not hesitate to authorize the participation of Bulgarian forces. In fact, he soon emerged as the Soviet bloc's most outspoken defender of the "Brezhnev doctrine"—the policy announced by Soviet leader Leonid Brezhnev that Warsaw Pact troops would be mobilized any time "the survival of socialism" was under attack. Bulgaria and the Soviet Union would always "act as a single body, breathing with the same lungs, and nourished by the same bloodstream,"[1] Zhivkov declared in 1973. And over the next decade, he would have little reason to reconsider the wisdom of his words.

Throughout the 1970s, Zhivkov remained firmly in control in Bulgaria. In 1976, he appointed his own daughter Ludmilla as the country's head of art and cultural affairs. Although her appointment had originally been seen as nothing more than favoritism, before too long Ludmilla—an outgoing and enthusiastic public speaker who cultivated an interest in subjects as diverse as Italian opera and Buddhist philosophy—was being hailed in the West as a "Communist breath of fresh air."

Then, in 1979, the Communist Party's Central Committee endorsed Zhivkov's proposal for a "New Economic Model" (N.E.M.) to modernize Bulgaria's economy. The N.E.M. promised, among other things, to bring democracy to Bulgaria's workplaces by allowing workers to elect their own leaders. There also were to be more and better consumer goods as well as a large increase in foreign trade.

Encouraged by the development of the N.E.M. and by the country's gradual emergence from isolation, many Bulgarians began to have a new sense of optimism about the future of their nation. However, their hopes would soon be dashed. Late in

Todor Zhivkov became the most powerful man within the Bulgarian Communist Party.

Ludmilla Zhivkova was appointed as the Bulgaria's head of art and cultural affairs.

1979 the Bulgarian government was embarrassed by reports that agents of its secret police, the notorious Department Six, had murdered an exiled Bulgarian writer, Georgi Markov, in London the previous September. The murder of Markov was only uncovered several months later, when Bulgarian agents attempted to kill another exile by means of the very same method they had used on Markov: "accidentally" stabbing him in the leg with a poison-tipped umbrella.

Soon there were also reports that agents from Department Six were involved in international drug trafficking and were being used to provide money and weapons to a wide range of international terrorists. Later, articles appeared in the world press linking the Bulgarian government to the attempt to assassinate Pope John Paul II in Rome in May 1981.

When Ludmilla Zhivkova died of a brain hemorrhage in July 1981, the entire country mourned the passing of a young, creative leader. Zhivkova was only 39 years old when she died. Soon there was other bad news for Bulgaria. For one, the N.E.M. was not living up to expectations that it would "remake

Bulgaria." Soaring energy costs had led to decreased production, which had led in turn to severe shortages of many everyday necessities. As a result, the Communist government decided to build a nationwide network of nuclear power plants. Following the nuclear accident at Chernobyl in the Ukraine in 1986, however, the Bulgarian program was halted. Then the standard of living for most Bulgarians began to decline steadily.

In addition, there was growing evidence that the close relationship between Bulgaria and the USSR was in decline. Following the death of the Soviet leader Leonid Brezhnev in 1982, Zhivkov had openly expressed his opinion that Brezhnev's close associate Konstantin Chernenko, rather than the reform-minded Yuri Andropov, should succeed Brezhnev. When the ruling Politburo of the Soviet Communist Party chose Andropov as their new leader, Bulgaria lost its place as the "closest friend" of the USSR. When Andropov died after little more than a year, Zhivkov again supported Chernenko, rather than an even younger reformer named Mikhail Gorbachev. This time, Chernenko was elected the Soviet party's general secretary. However, in 13 months, Chernenko too was dead, and the way was cleared for Gorbachev.

In July 1985, Zhivkov traveled to Moscow for the first time since Chernenko's funeral four months before. As a sign of his displeasure with the Bulgarian leader's past meddling in Soviet affairs, Gorbachev refused to find time to meet with Zhivkov for two full days—until the eve of Zhivkov's return to Sofia. A little while later, the Soviet ambassador to Bulgaria told a newspaper reporter that while the roots connecting Bulgaria and the Soviet Union were still strong, the tree of friendship between the two countries nevertheless needed watering from time to time if it was to bear fruit. Bulgaria's past record of unquestioned loyalty to the Soviet Union clearly counted for very little in the new age of Gorbachev and *perestroika*.

A family of Bulgarian Turks leaving Bulgaria with their belongings

As 1989 wore on, one old-time Communist leader after another resigned under the pressure of change—first Janos Kadar in Hungary, then Erich Honecker in East Germany—and as fall arrived it became apparent that not even Bulgaria's isolation could keep Todor Zhivkov in power.

Since the Communist takeover in 1947, very few Bulgarians had dared to speak out against their government. The Zhivkov government had brutally put down all hints of opposition by the country's largest minority group, 1.5 million ethnic Turks, who composed nearly one fifth of the country's entire population. In 1984 the

Communist authorities instituted a program of "Bulgarianization" in the country's southern provinces. The use of the Turkish language in public was prohibited, as was the open practice of the Islamic religion. Turkish villages were given new Bulgarian names, and the government commanded nearly a million ethnic Turks to change their Turkish names into Bulgarian ones.

Time and again, the Bulgarian army would come into a Turkish village, usually in the middle of the night, and rouse the head of every household. He would then be forced to sign a government document listing the officially approved Bulgarian name of every family member. Those who refused to sign were beaten or were forced to watch as soldiers abused their wives and children. Thousands who still refused to sign were imprisoned and tortured; hundreds were eventually executed. The Bulgarian Communists also encouraged ethnic Turks to leave the country, and during the summer of 1989, more than 300,000 Bulgarian Turks fled across the border to Turkey. Finally overwhelmed by this massive movement of refugees, the Turkish government was forced to close its border with Bulgaria.

Occasionally a slight hint of an organized opposition to the Communists managed to surface within Bulgaria. In March 1978, "Declaration 78," a proclamation demanding human rights, was smuggled out of the country and published in the West. Also from time to time—most recently in May 1989—the Sofia police were called in to arrest a few dozen men and women demonstrating outside of government offices in Sofia.

In October 1989, Sofia was selected to host an international meeting of UNESCO (the United Nations Educational, Scientific and Cultural Organization). A number of foreign reporters were assigned to cover the story. For a few days, Bulgaria would be the focus of more of the world's attention than usual. Because of this exposure, the members of a small Bulgarian environmental group, Eco-Glasnost, decided it would be a good time for a public demonstration.

On the morning of November 3, several hundred members and supporters of Eco-Glasnost gathered in a large park in the center of Sofia. As they left the park and turned to march toward the National Assembly building, they were already crossing a historic threshold in their country's recent history. For the first time in over 40 years, a public demonstration against the government was being held in the streets of the Bulgarian capital. As the line of march proceeded through the center of the city, hundreds more—then thousands—joined in. By the time they reached the large square in front of the hall where the UNESCO conference was taking place, several thousand men and women had dared to assemble openly to protest the damage the Communists' policies had done to the Bulgarian environment. They demanded an end to poorly considered projects that upset the natural balance, the dismantling of the country's nuclear power plants, modernization of old factories that belched poisonous fumes into the air and poured harmful chemicals into the country's waterways, and stricter air pollution standards for Sofia and other large cities.

As the crowd grew larger, other demands were heard as well—for political reform, human rights, and an end to all government attempts to "Bulgarianize" the ethnic Turks. But the loudest cries of all that day were those demanding that Todor Zhivkov resign.

Still the authorities made no move to halt the demonstrations. Perhaps Zhivkov was unwilling to send troops against his own people before the eyes of hundreds of UNESCO delegates, who were watching from the windows of their meeting hall. Perhaps he feared such action would become the featured news story around the world that day, merely reinforcing the world's idea of Bulgaria as an isolated, hopelessly backward land. No, the Bulgarian authorities decided, the Eco-Glasnost demonstration would be allowed to continue. The protesters would be allowed to have their say—and then go home.

Many Bulgarians feared that once the UNESCO conference was over and the foreign press had left the country, Zhivkov would move ruthlessly to crush the small, weak opposition. But now thousands of other Bulgarians felt freed at last from the fear that had held them in check for more than 40 years. On November 9, as news arrived from Germany that the Berlin Wall had been opened, perhaps 100,000 people were gathering in the streets of Sofia to demand that their country too must change. "Resign!" the crowd shouted. "Zhivkov must go!" Some held aloft official photographs of their 78-year-old leader, the man who had ruled longer than any other Communist Party chief in Europe. Over Zhivkov's stern and serious face, the demonstrators painted prison bars or Nazi swastikas. There were demands for Zhivkov's arrest and trial on charges of corruption. Others demanded that the hated Department Six security police be disbanded and that those responsible for the persecution of Bulgaria's Turkish minority be brought to justice.

Finally the need for change became apparent, even within the highest levels of the Communist Party. Bulgaria's foreign minister, Petar Mladenov, met with the old party boss early on the morning of November 10 and forthrightly told Zhivkov that he no longer had a choice: He must resign. The crowds were already gathering in the central square for another day of demonstrations, Mladenov said. They would grow larger every day, until Zhivkov finally gave in and stepped down. The only way the Communists could hope to regain the confidence of the people was for Mladenov to replace Zhivkov as head of the party.

Mladenov told his longtime superior that he had already polled the ruling Politburo. A clear majority was now willing to vote to remove Zhivkov from power, if necessary.

Zhivkov agreed that he had already remained in power too long. Perhaps, he said, he should have retired 10 years before. He would not cling any longer. An emergency meeting of the Politburo was convened. There, Zhivkov formally announced his "retirement" as general secretary of the Communist Party.

▼ ▲ ▼

Mladenov moved quickly to demonstrate his commitment to genuine political reform. "We have to turn Bulgaria into a modern, democratic, and lawful country," he declared. "There is no alternative to *perestroika*."[2] Within a week of coming to power, Mladenov expressed his support for the idea of allowing other political parties to compete in genuinely free elections. A month later, on December 11, 1989, the Communist-controlled National Assembly scheduled elections for May of the next year. It also lifted the ban on the formation of non-Communist political groups and even removed references in the nations' constitution to the "leading role" of the Communist Party in Bulgarian society.

Perhaps, many Bulgarians thought, the country was truly on the road at last toward genuine freedom and democracy. Certainly it would be a long and difficult road. Although Mladenov represented some improvement over Zhivkov, he was still a Communist, and a dedicated party member at that. The Communists still had control of the nation's political structure, economy, foreign relations, and news media. The non-Communist opposition was small, weak, and disunited. Yet, as 1989 came to an end, many Bulgarians dared to speak openly of electing a non-Communist president sometime in the near future. And, as the new decade of the 1990s began, many Bulgarians dared to hope that their country's long and troubled Communist sleep was drawing to a close at last.

prague: The Velvet Revolution

On the morning of November 17, 1989, tens of thousands of people—almost all of them students—packed a large Jewish cemetery in the Old Town of Czechoslovakia's capital, Prague. Somewhat to their surprise, their student organization had been granted permission by the government to hold a brief ceremony in memory of Jan Opletal, a Jewish student killed by the Nazis almost 50 years before.

Most of those present in the huge crowd could not see or hear the ceremony that was taking place by the young martyr's grave. But most of those present that morning were there not only to remember past events but also to make sure that Czechoslovakia too was caught up in the tide of change that was now sweeping over Central and Eastern Europe.

As soon as the ceremony at Opletal's grave was over, some of the demonstrators began chanting slogans against the Communist government of President Gustav Husák. Others began to sing "We Shall Overcome." The cry that filled the air most often was "Svodoba! Freedom!"

The crowd moved on, beyond the cemetery, then out of the Old District, past the historic Charles Bridge, and along the embankment of the Vltava River. It took a turn at the National Theater onto Národni Třida (Avenue of the People), and then finally into Wenceslas Square—the very center of Prague, where so many important events in the country's history had taken place. In Wenceslas Square invading Warsaw Pact troops had crushed the Prague Spring reform movement and its hopes of "socialism with a human face" 21 years before.

When the students arrived at the square, riot police were waiting for them. The government had also mobilized a special antiterrorist squadron, wearing red berets to differentiate them from the regular soldiers. Those in the front lines of the march tried to hand bunches of flowers to the police. Others placed lighted candles on the ground, then held up their arms and announced, "We have bare hands. We are not armed."[1]

Quickly, however, the security forces made their move. One brigade was dispatched to the end of the avenue leading into the

Student demonstrators gathered in Wenceslas Square place lighted candles on the ground.

square, preventing the escape of any marchers who might try to flee. Waving their weapons, the Red Berets marched directly into the line of protesters. Row after row of unarmed civilians fell to the ground. As each row fell, the police trampled right over them and moved straight ahead, ready to pummel the next row of victims. Then the police fired tear gas canisters to clear any stragglers from the area. Within minutes, not a single soul remained standing in Wenceslas Square. One student lay dead, and Prague's hospitals soon filled with the hundreds of others who had been injured.

Early the next day—Saturday, November 18—students at various schools throughout the capital voted to call a strike. That afternoon the actors' union became the first organization openly to side with the students. A mass meeting of students and actors was held at the Realistic Theater. One speaker after another rose to speak against the "massacre of November 17." Then a decision was reached: There would be a general strike exactly one week later, on November 27. All the people of the country would be given the chance to stand up against police brutality and in support of human rights.

The next evening, representatives of several dissident groups met at another Prague theater and agreed to form a common organization to coordinate opposition to the government. They called their new organization Civic Forum and chose the human rights activist Václav Havel to serve as their chief spokesperson. Havel, one of Czechoslovakia's leading playwrights, had long been a critic of the country's Communist government. He was a leader of Charter 77, Czechoslovakia's leading human rights organization, and had been imprisoned for several years for his dissident activities. While Civic Forum was being organized in Prague, a similar group, Public Against Violence, was being formed in Bratislava to lead the democratic movement in Slovakia.

Over the weekend, tens of thousands of students gathered in Wenceslas Square. In spite of the seriousness of the event, the atmosphere was high-spirited, almost festive. Groups of students climbed atop the mounted statue of King Wenceslas. Walls along the square were hung with brightly colored banners and murals. Throughout the weekend, the crowds grew even larger. By Monday, it was obvious that the gathering was more than just another student protest. People of all ages and occupations jammed the square, and the tens of thousands became hundreds of thousands. Their shouts—"Freedom!" "Resign!" "Now is the time!"—shook the centuries-old, baroque-styled buildings in the heart of the capital.

Throughout the next day, Tuesday, the crowd continued to swell steadily, finally reaching its peak in the late afternoon, when workers leaving their jobs headed straight to the demonstrations. Prague's subway line was packed. Everyone, it seemed, was heading toward Wenceslas Square. Soon the square looked like an ocean of people, with barely a single square inch unoccupied. That afternoon Václav Havel addressed the crowd for the first time, speaking from a balcony overlooking the square. Havel repeated the Civil Forum's main demands and reminded the crowd of the general strike, now just three days away. A new cry—"Strike! Strike!"—shook the square.

▼ ▲ ▼

In his office at Prague Castle, President Husák heard the latest reports of the demonstrations. In spite of the rise of Gorbachev in the Soviet Union, Husák had always maintained that there would be no radical reforms in socialist Czechoslovakia. But his government was completely unprepared for this turn of events. Somehow, through Wednesday and Thursday, the crowds continued to grow. Now there were half a million or more demonstrators crowding the center of Prague. Police units—even the antiterrorist squads—would be no match for such masses of people. And, Husák knew, there would be no assistance from the Warsaw Pact this time. Gorbachev had been very clear about one thing on his last visit to Czechoslovakia: Relations between the Czechoslovak government and its critics would now be viewed by Moscow as a strictly internal matter. The Czechs and Slovaks would have to solve their own problems.

Husák considered the options remaining open to him. Perhaps he could send in the army. Armed infantry, even tanks, could drive right into the heart of Prague to clear the square. The loss of life would be terrible. Blood would flow in the streets. It would be Tiananmen all over again—in the very heart of Europe. And the entire scene would be televised around the world. There would be screams of protest, and Husák would be viewed as an international criminal. Czechoslovakia would come to be seen as an outlaw state in the eyes of the world. No, Gustav Husák conceded, there was nothing the government could do now but offer to negotiate with the protesters.

The Czechoslovak prime minister, Ladislav Adamec, sent a representative to the Magic Lantern Theater, where Civic Forum had set up its headquarters. Adamec was willing to meet with an opposition delegation the next day, the courier said. But the prime minister was adamant that the delegation *not* include Václav Havel. The Communists were not yet ready to meet with a man long portrayed as a chief enemy of the state.

The next morning, a government limousine arrived at the Magic Lantern to transport the Civil Forum delegation to the prime minister's office in Prague Castle. Havel accompanied them to the castle but was forbidden from entering the prime minister's office. At first the other Civic Forum representatives hesitated; they insisted that Havel, too, be allowed to take part in the negotiations. But Havel told them to go ahead into the prime minister's office; this was too important an opportunity for the Forum to waste. He would remain behind in the lobby and chat with other visitors to the castle. Reluctantly the rest of the Civil Forum representatives agreed to negotiate without Havel. A group calling itself The Bridge was formed to relay Adamec's comments back to Havel in the lobby as well as to communicate Havel's views to those negotiating upstairs.

▼ ▲ ▼

On November 24, Alexander Dubček, the leader of the 1968
Prague Spring movement, returned to the Czechoslovak capital.
Accompanied by Havel, he made his way to Wenceslas Square.
The crowd below erupted in a thunderous roar as Havel and
Dubček, heroes of two different generations, appeared on the
balcony. Even though it was a cold, gray November afternoon,
the hopes of that spring 21 years before—hopes of freedom and
democracy—were coming to flower again in Prague.

Dubček and Havel then returned to the Magic Lantern, where
representatives of the world's news media were eager to ask
them questions. The press conference had barely begun when a
courier arrived with amazing news: The entire Politburo of the
Communist Party had just announced its resignation! It was
now obvious that the Communists were in complete disarray. On
stage, before the eyes of the world, Havel and Dubček embraced
warmly. A bottle of champagne was produced, and a toast was
offered "to a free Czechoslovakia!"[2]

Two days later, on November 26, a second delegation from
Civic Forum met with Prime Minister Adamec. This time the delegation was led by Václav Havel. After long and difficult
negotiations, Adamec finally agreed that all political prisoners
would be released immediately. The government followed
through on this promise, and that evening some of the released
prisoners made their way to Prague and the Magic Lantern to
take part in Civic Forum's deliberations. Havel had refused to
give in to the government's pleading that the general strike scheduled for the next day be postponed. It would go on as planned.

On the morning of Monday, November 27, business in most
establishments around Prague seemed to go on as usual. However,
just before noon the atmosphere in the city changed noticeably.
Shopkeepers drew the shutters on their windows and hung
"Closed" signs on their doors. Factory workers put down their
tools, put on their jackets, and walked outside into the cold

November air. The Prague subway came to a halt, as did the inner-city bus lines. Taxicab drivers pulled over to the curb. At just one minute before noon, the anchorman on state television announced that he too was joining the strike. In full view of the television cameras, he rose from his seat and walked off the set. Replacing him on screen was a group of technicians in Wenceslas Square, announcing that instead of stopping work, they would show their support for the strike by broadcasting it live across the country!

During a two-hour general strike, a young Czech boy waves his country's flag while standing next to a statue of former Soviet leader Joseph Stalin in Prague's Wenceslas Square. The poster says "Never Forever."

At exactly noon the general strike began. Prague, usually an active, noisy city of one and a quarter million people, was given over to peace and quiet. The scene was repeated in cities across the land—in Brno, Ostrava, and Bratislava. From one end of Czechoslovakia to the other, the general strike was an overwhelming success. Millions of Czechs and Slovaks took part, and for two hours the country came to a virtual standstill.

The next day, following a brief meeting with a delegation from Civic Forum, Adamec issued a statement declaring that a new government composed of a "broad coalition" of parties would be formed within five days. However, the broad coalition offered by the government proved completely unacceptable. Of 21 posts in the new government, 16 would still be held by Communists, many of them well-known supporters of Husák's hard-line policies. Civic Forum immediately rejected the government's offer.

The mood of the demonstrators in Wenceslas Square became increasingly defiant. When they heard of Adamec's proposals for a "broad coalition," the shout "Resign!" rose from the crowd as though it was speaking in one voice. Other demonstrators sneered at the five positions reserved for non-Communists in the new government and took up the cry "Five crumbs won't feed us!" Others responded, "We are here to stay!"[3]

One morning a large group of students dressed as Santa Claus (or as Saint Nicholas, as he is known in Czechoslovakia) gathered outside the main headquarters of the Communist Party. Instead of delivering presents to the party leaders however, they dumped large bags of garbage in front of the headquarters! The next morning, another group of students constructed a wall of cardboard boxes 15 feet high in front of the offices of various government ministries. Many government workers on their way to their jobs gave up trying to find a way around the wall and returned home instead.

▼ ▲ ▼

On Thursday, December 7, Ladislav Adamec was replaced as Czechoslovakia's prime minister by a young reform Communist named Márian Calfa. Calfa's first action in office was to invite representatives of Civic Forum and Public Against Violence to reopen negotiations with the government. The opposition accepted Calfa's offer, and a delegation led by Havel left immediately for the castle. After a short negotiating session, an agreement was reached.

Calfa would remain as the country's prime minister until genuinely free elections could be held, sometime in the spring of 1990. A new government would be formed immediately, in which Civic Forum and Public Against Violence would hold seven positions and the Communists would hold only ten. (Two of the Communists were reform Communists who were also members of Civic Forum.) The Socialist and People's parties—former allies of the Communists who were now sympathetic to the opposition— would hold two positions each. Calfa would also share control of the interior ministry with two Forum members, Valtr Komarek and Jan Čarnogursky, who would also serve as vice premiers. Just days before, Čarnogursky had been on trial in Bratislava, charged with undermining the government. He had been found guilty, of course, and was awaiting sentencing when word arrived that all political prisoners were to be released. Čarnogursky hurried straight from jail to the Magic Lantern. Now, he was to be one of three men in charge of the state security police!

That evening, Havel read the names of the new government to a jubilant crowd in the square. As each name was read, a great cheer went up from the hundreds of thousands of people gathered below. Men whom the government had held in utter contempt only weeks before now *were* the government. So much had changed so quickly. A revolution had swept over Czechoslovakia—a revolution of students and actors and writers and teachers and factory

workers and store clerks, a revolution completely without violence. Indeed the change in Czechoslovakia had been achieved so
gently and gracefully that people the world over began to refer to
it as the Velvet Revolution.

To many of the revolutionaries in Prague, one goal still
remained to be realized. Many people had begun to wear buttons
that read, "Havel for President." At nearly every mass rally the
cry "Havel na Hrad! Havel to the Castle!" filled the air.

On December 10, the cabinet of the new coalition government
was sworn in at Prague Castle by the president of the Socialist
Republic of Czechoslovakia, Gustav Husák. For the first time in
41 years, non-Communists held a majority in the nation's
highest council. As soon as the ceremony was finished, one of the
new officials, Jiří Dienstbier, excused himself and went to find a
telephone. He had been in prison and during the years since his
release he had not been able to find work in his chosen field as a
journalist. Instead he had supported his family by working as a
boiler-room watchman. Now he was foreign minister of his
country. But as he was taking the oath of office, he realized that
he had forgotten to arrange for someone to check the boilers
that afternoon!

When Husák finished swearing in the new cabinet, he retired to
his office deep in one of the castle's many wings. There he put his
signature on his letter of resignation. He knew that there would be
no place for him in the government of a free Czechoslovakia.

▼ ▲ ▼

Attention now turned to the selection of a new president.
There was little doubt that Václav Havel would be Civic Forum's
nominee for the position. At first, some believed that the presidency should be offered to Alexander Dubček. However,
although almost all agreed that Dubček was an admirable and
honest man, many nevertheless also believed that his time in
history was past. The Velvet Revolution no longer sought merely

to reform the Communist system. The people who gathered in Wenceslas Square in the winter of 1989 would not be satisfied now unless the system was completely dismantled.

On the evening of December 16, Havel and Dubček met together and worked out an agreement. They both agreed that it was now time for Havel to become Czechoslovakia's new president. Havel insisted, however, that Dubček be named chairman of the National Assembly.

On December 28, the National Assembly, by a vote of 298 to 0, with 1 abstention, elected Alexander Dubček as its chairman. The next day, Prime Minister Calfa appeared before the assembly to place the name of Václav Havel in nomination for the presidency of Czechoslovakia. "He has won the respect of us all," Calfa said. "He never accepted the suggestions of friends or foes that he go into exile, and bore the humiliation of a man oppressed and relegated by those in power to the margins of society." Then the prime minister concluded, "Your vote for Václav Havel will be a vote for insuring the human rights of every citizen of our country."[4]

The members of the National Assembly then cast their ballots. Though there was never any doubt as to the result of the voting, the chamber nevertheless grew quiet as the clerk prepared to announce the tally. All 323 votes cast in the National Assembly that day were in favor of Václav Havel's candidacy. Havel would be the new president of the Czechoslovak Socialist Republic.

Alexander Dubček administered the oath of office. The words Havel read were almost exactly the same as those Husák had spoken on assuming the presidency in 1975. Havel promised to obey the constitution and the laws of the republic, to watch over the interests of the Czechoslovak people, and to administer the duties of his office with fairness and equity. However, unlike Husák, Havel did not have to swear "to defend socialism against all enemies." Just the day before, the National Assembly had voted to delete that clause from the presidential oath.

Václav Havel flashes the victory sign to thousands of Czechs after he was elected president of Czechoslovakia.

When the swearing in was completed, Olga Havel joined her husband in the plaza outside Prague Castle. There an army unit fired a 20-gun salute in honor of the country's new president. The unit then stood at attention, arms presented, before their new leader. Slowly, deliberately, Havel passed before them in review. The gentle-mannered, intellectual playwright was now the commander in chief of the armed forces of Czechoslovakia.

That evening, the streets of Prague were filled with people celebrating the victory of the Velvet Revolution. All across the city, people danced in the streets and sang patriotic songs as loudly as they could. That night the sounds of once-forbidden rock and roll shook the windows around Wenceslas Square. Russian champagne flowed freely as numerous toasts were offered: "To Havel! To freedom! To democracy! To Czechoslovakia!" Many people said that the country had never seen such a grand party.

▼ ▲ ▼

In the midst of the great tide of change that swept over the face of Europe during 1989, the British writer Timothy Garton Ash made an observation that was widely quoted as one revolution seemed to give way quickly to the next, all across Central and Eastern Europe: "In Poland, the revolution took ten years," Ash remarked. "In Hungary, it took ten months; in Germany, ten weeks." During the Velvet Revolution, another phrase was added: "In Czechoslovakia, ten days."[5]

In reality, of course, the Velvet Revolution took somewhat longer than that: a little more than a month from start to finish. But still, as Havel would later tell the United States Congress, the old political speedometers were no longer adequate. The world was changing more rapidly than most would have imagined possible just a short time before.

chapter 9

Bucharest: Death of a Dictator

A s the thin, rather drawn-looking man at the podium concluded his speech, the audience leapt to their feet and applauded enthusiastically. Then they began to chant in rhythm to their clapping: "Ceau-şes-cu! Ceau-şes-cu!" After a while, they shouted different slogans: first, "Ceauşescu and Romania!" then, "Ceauşescu and socialism!" and finally, "Ceauşescu and victory!" Through all this, their leader stood before them, nodding his head, waving stiffly to the crowd, a tight smile seemingly pasted onto his face. After a few minutes, he was joined on the platform by a woman of similar stature and manner. She was wearing a dark blue suit and a white, ruffled blouse. Her hair was drawn back into a tight bun, which seemed only to accentuate the thin, sharp features of her face.

Soon the pair seemed to grow tired of the admiring crowd. The man motioned to the crowd to sit and he and the woman turned to take their seats at the side of the podium. In an instant the applause stopped, and the obedient delegates sat down once again.

Thus on November 23, 1989, Nicolae Ceauşescu was reelected general secretary of the Communist Party of Romania. In his speech before the party congress, Ceauşescu had pledged that in spite of the great political changes that had swept across Eastern Europe, Romania would never turn away from the true Communist path.

Nicolae Ceauşescu waves to cheering delegates of the Congress of the Communist Party in Bucharest.

▼ ▲ ▼

Ceauşescu had become the head of the Communist Party of Romania in 1965. Almost immediately, he sought to establish himself as a Communist leader who was dedicated to reform and modernization. Following his refusal to allow Romanian troops to take part in the Warsaw Pact's invasion of Czechoslovakia in 1968, many observers declared that Ceauşescu had become "the West's favorite Communist." Beneath the surface, however, Ceauşescu was a brutal dictator, and the Romanian people suffered terribly under him.

In 1971, Ceauşescu traveled to China and North Korea. On this trip the Romanian leader was favorably impressed by Chairman Mao Zedong's "Cultural Revolution," which sought to "purify" Chinese Communism and rid it of all Western ideas. Ceauşescu also admired the "personality cult" created for the North Korean Communist leader Kim Il Sung. It set the leader high on a pedestal to be worshipped by his people.

When Ceauşescu returned to Bucharest from his trip to Asia, he declared that a new "Era of Light" was about to begin in Romania. All would-be reformers were removed from high party positions, and Ceauşescu named dozens of his own friends and relatives in their places. Although she had not even graduated from high school, the dictator's wife, Elena, was granted the title Doctor of Science and was named director of the nation's Academy of Sciences! Later she would also become a member of the Communist Party's ruling Politburo and take the office of first deputy prime minister. It was also widely assumed that the Ceauşescus' son, Niku, would succeed his father as Romania's leader.

Soon portraits of Ceauşescu were hung in public buildings and city squares throughout the land. The state-controlled press declared him the "Greatest Son of the Romanian People," "Wise Helmsman of the Ship of State," and even "Chosen Titan Among Titans." Elena was called Ceauşescu's "Most Esteemed and Closest Colleague," the "Shining Symbol of the National Spirit," and a "Scientific Genius." In 1974 the office of president of Romania was established, to which Ceauşescu, of course, was unanimously elected. Yet, in spite of all the titles bestowed on him, Ceauşescu preferred to be known simply as the "Conducator" or "Leader"—the conductor of the nation's destiny.

Ceauşescu used his position as "the West's favorite Communist" to gain billions of dollars in loans and credits from foreign banks and governments. He frittered away much of this economic assistance on large, poorly considered public works projects. More than a billion dollars were used to build a little-used shipping port at Constanta, on the Black Sea. Two billion dollars more were spent to construct a canal connecting Constanta with Cernadova on the Danube River.

By 1982, Romania's foreign debt had grown to more than $22 billion, one of the highest in the world. Ceauşescu then decreed that Romania would repay all the money it owed by 1990, almost 10 years ahead of schedule. To meet this new timetable, Ceauşescu ordered the export of virtually anything that could be sold abroad. Prior to World War II, Romania had been known as the "breadbasket" of Eastern Europe, supplying much of the continent with cattle, corn, and wheat. Now, Romanians would be forced to do without the basic necessities of life so that their dictator's grand scheme could be realized. Overnight, it seemed, items such as chocolate and fresh fruit disappeared from store shelves. Strict rationing was imposed on most other food items.

To save fuel, residents of Bucharest were forbidden to heat their apartments to a temperature higher than 52 degrees Fahrenheit, even in the middle of winter. Apartments were limited to a single 40-watt light bulb, and in cities and towns across the country, electricity and hot water were turned on only for a few hours each day.

Late in 1983, Ceauşescu gave the order to level most of the historic Old District of Bucharest so that he might build in its place a mammoth complex of modern government buildings.

Construction of the Avenue of the Victory of Socialism in Bucharest

More than 50,000 residents of the capital were given just 48 hours' notice to vacate their homes. Tens of thousands of historical old buildings, including dozens of centuries-old churches, synagogues, marketplaces, and theaters were bulldozed into the ground to make way for the new Avenue of the Victory of Socialism, which stretched for two miles into the heart of the capital. Along its entire length, the avenue was lined with hastily constructed concrete government offices and apartment houses.

At the very end of the Avenue of Victory was to be the crowning monument to Ceauşescu's Era of Light: the solid marble House of the Republic, which was 330 feet tall, 720 feet wide, and 840 feet long. Between 1984 and 1989, as many as 15,000 people a day worked on the project, and at least 20 lives were lost in the process. The construction costs of the building rose to more than a billion dollars and drained the country's entire supply of lumber, marble, and glass. The huge chandeliers in Ceauşescu's office alone consumed the same amount of electricity as 350 four-room apartments.

▼ ▲ ▼

By the mid-1980s, the ill-considered policies of the Ceauşescu regime had pushed Romania to the brink of bankruptcy and despair. Yet Ceauşescu seemed as determined as ever to press ahead with his mad design. Early in 1988, he announced a program to "systematize" life in the country's rural areas. More than 7,000 of Romania's 13,000 villages were to be destroyed, and their inhabitants sent to live in modern concrete and cinder-block "agricultural-industrial complexes" far from their original homes. Most of the villages slated for destruction were located in Romania's westernmost region, Transylvania.

The fate of Transylvania had long been a source of conflict between Romania and neighboring Hungary. Control of the region had passed to Romania at the close of World War I, but Nazi Germany had returned Transylvania to Hungary in 1940 in exchange for Hungarian support in World War II. Then, following the defeat of Germany and its allies in 1945, the region once again became part of Romania. Many believed that Ceauşescu's "systemi-zation" program was actually an attempt to destroy the culture of the 2 million ethnic Hungarians who lived in Transylvania and to bring them under the complete control of Bucharest.

People the world over were outraged by Ceauşescu's plan. By the summer of 1988, tensions between the Communist "allies" Hungary and Romania had so heightened that the border between the two states was closed. Earlier, on a state visit to Romania, Mikhail Gorbachev had issued a stern public warning to Ceauşescu. "Human beings cannot be treated as gears in a machine," Gorbachev told the Romanian dictator.[1] But Ceauşescu did not seem to be listening. Instead, he continued to insist that the systemization program would be carried out as scheduled.

But if the Romanian tyrant seemed unimpressed by the changes going on elsewhere in the world, the same could not be said of an increasing number of Romania's people. In August 1989, a videotaped interview with Laszlo Tökes, the

minister of the Hungarian Reformed Church in the
Transylvanian city of Timişoara, was shown on Hungarian
television. In the interview, Tökes declared that Ceauşescu's
systemization amounted to nothing less than "cultural genocide" against the Hungarians in Romania. The program must
be halted at all costs.

In response to the interview, Romanian authorities confiscated
Tökes's ration book. Without it, he would be unable to purchase
basic necessities such as bread, meat, and fuel. The telephone
line to Tökes's home was cut, and visitors who tried to bring
food to him and his family were turned away by the police. In
early November, masked thugs broke into Tökes's home and
beat and stabbed him. Every window in the house was broken,
as were all of the windows of Tökes's church down the street.
Still the young minister refused to silence his criticisms of the
Communist regime.

Finally the government ordered Tökes's own bishop to reas-
sign him to a different church, in the south of the country.
When Tökes defied his own superior's command to move, the
bishop obtained a court order to evict Tökes from his house
and on December 15 appealed to the police for assistance. But
before the police could arrive, hundreds of citizens of
Timişoara—men, women and children, young and old,
Hungarians and Romanians alike—surrounded Tökes's house,
forming a human chain to prevent the police from evicting the
young minister.

The police quickly fled in the face of the huge crowd.
Emboldened by their victory, hundreds gathered again the next
day and marched to the center of Timişoara. Now the crowd
shouted defiant slogans: "Down with the ration cards! Down
with systemization! Down with the dictatorship!" When the
crowd reached the Communist Party headquarters, control
broke down. Rocks and bottles were thrown, and windows were
smashed. After several hours, police armed with water cannons
and tear gas managed to restore an uneasy calm.

Lazlo Tökes in his vandalized church

▼ ▲ ▼

When word of the demonstration in Timişoara reached
Ceauşescu, he became enraged. This was evidence of a plot by
Washington and Moscow to bring him down, he screamed. Why
hadn't the police been given orders to use deadly force against
such "traitors and hooligans"? When the minister of defense,
Vasile Milea, and General Iulian Vlad, the commander of the
state security police, the Securitate, tried to reason with
Ceauşescu, his anger only increased. They were traitors as well,
Ceauşescu roared. It was their fault that the situation had gotten
out of hand. "A few hooligans want to destroy socialism, and
you make it child's play for them!" the dictator shrieked.[2] No,
Ceauşescu commanded, it would not be enough for Vlad and
Milea simply to resign. Rather, they should be put before a
firing squad and shot! If they were not, Ceauşescu warned, then
he himself would resign.

Elena Ceauşescu tried to calm her husband. "The country
needs you, Nik," she pleaded. "We could not survive without
you!"[3] Milea and Vlad and several other members of the
Politburo then dropped to their knees, begging Ceauşescu not to
resign. Tearfully they apologized for their mistakes and asked
the Conducator to give them one more chance. They promised
they would do whatever he ordered to bring the situation under
control. Finally Ceauşescu agreed not to resign. But, he insisted,
any further antigovernment demonstrators must be dealt with
firmly. All units of the interior ministry, the militia, security
troops, and Romanian border guards were to be armed with
combat weapons, loaded with live ammunition. Anyone who dis-
obeyed orders to go on their way or who attempted to destroy
government property would be shot on sight.

Ceauşescu then dispatched several senior government ministers, including Prime Minister Constantin Dascalescu, to
Timişoara to supervise the suppression of the "insurrection." He
also appointed General Ion Coman as commander of all forces in

Timişoara. Ceauşescu ordered Coman to restore calm to Timişoara as quickly as possible.

Within hours, three columns of heavily armed troops were marching into the center of the Transylvanian city. When the troops were in place, a voice over a loudspeaker ordered all private citizens to return to their homes peacefully. When the crowd refused to move, a round of warning shots were fired into the air. But the men and women of Timişoara still refused to flee. They stood firmly in their places, still shouting their slogans at the top of their voices. "Down with Ceauşescu!" they shouted. "Down with the dictatorship!" They even taunted the troops with shouts of "Ceauşescu, come and get us!"

The troops opened fire. A row of children standing at the front of the line scrambled for cover in a nearby church. Three army officers who refused to follow their commander's order to fire into the crowd were shot dead at point-blank range by agents of the Securitate. The buildings around Timişoara's central square disappeared in a haze of dust and smoke. Blood stained the cobblestone streets as hundreds fell to the ground.

The next day, December 18, Ceauşescu left as planned for a state visit to Iran. He had received the latest reports from Transylvania and was now satisfied that his orders were being carried out. Word of the massacre in Timişoara spread quickly from one end of Romania to the other. Reports of the number killed ranged from several dozen to over 5,000. (Later reports would put the actual number at around 100.) By the next day, striking workers in several Romanian cities were threatening to blow up their factories unless Ceauşescu stepped down. There were reports of demonstrations in Sibiu, Brasov, and several other large cities. University students in Bucharest had begun holding meetings to discuss the situation in the country. And in Timişoara itself, the men and women who had survived the massacre of December 17 were in the streets again the next day, demanding the return of the bodies of those who had been killed. Cries of "Down with Ceauşescu!" were now mingled with cries of "Give us our dead!"

Ceauşescu returned from Iran two days later still convinced of his ability to maintain control. Within a few hours of landing at Otopeni Airport outside Bucharest, the dictator delivered a televised address to the nation. Looking stern and angry, flanked on both sides by the grim-faced Elena and a few trusted officials, Ceauşescu repeated his theory that the trouble in Timişoara had been caused by "fascist agents" who wanted to sever Transylvania from Romania. The very independence of the country was at stake, Ceauşescu declared, and he would not give in to the enemies of socialism. No, Ceauşescu bellowed, there would be no change of government in Romania "until pears grow on poplar trees."[4]

Late that night, under the cover of darkness, students at Bucharest University crept out of their dormitories to the center of the college campus. They used packing twine to attach large green pears to the branches of the poplar trees that had grown there for years. When the people of Bucharest awoke the next morning, word quickly spread that however confident the Conducator had appeared the night before, pears were in fact "growing" on poplar trees in the Romanian capital!

▼ ▲ ▼

Ceauşescu had also demanded that a massive demonstration be held in the square in front of the headquarters of the Communist Party in Bucharest the next day. This, he said, would give the Romanian people the opportunity to demonstrate to the entire world the high esteem they had for their leader. Ceauşescu also insisted that the rally be broadcast live on Romanian National Television.

Early in the afternoon of December 21, thousands of hand-picked workers from particular factories, shops, and offices throughout the Romanian capital were loaded onto buses and taken to Gheorghiu-Dej Square in front of the Central Committee building. There, Communist Party officials told them where to stand and which slogans to shout. When the rally was finished, the demonstrators would be bused back to their places of work.

At first, the rally on December 21 proceeded as planned. Ceauşescu appeared on the balcony, dressed in a heavy woolen coat and a black fur hat against the winter cold. To the dictator's left stood his wife, Elena, and General Vlad of the Securitate. To his right stood the same high-ranking government ministers who had appeared with him as he had delivered his television address the night before. As Ceauşescu and his entourage appeared, a loud cheer came forth from the crowd. Some had been given Romanian flags or large banners. Others held high their portraits of the "Greatest Son of the Romanian people" and his "Most Esteemed and Closest Colleague."

However, even as Ceauşescu began to speak, another group of demonstrators was making its way to the capital's central square. Hundreds of students from Bucharest University, intent on demanding a full investigation of the massacre in Timişoara, had left their college campus just a short while before. As the students approached Gheorghiu-Dej Square, they were surprised to discover the pro-government rally already underway, and Ceauşescu himself addressing the crowd! Now, the students knew, the opportunity was at hand to let the dictator know how they felt.

In his speech, Ceauşescu repeated the main points he had made the previous evening. The fascists were at work in Timişoara, Ceauşescu screeched. Fascists and imperialists were intent upon tearing Romania apart. They wanted to bring back capitalism, bring back oppression of the working class, bring back unemployment. But he—Ceauşescu—and the heroic Romanian people would never let that happen.

On cue, the party-organized crowd cheered and began to chant the dictator's name. But when Ceauşescu started to speak again about the "Hungarian agents" who were stirring up trouble in Transylvania, there was a loud crackling sound—gunfire—or perhaps a firecracker. Then, from the back of the assembled crowd, a loud scream arose. Startled, Ceauşescu looked up from the speech he was reading and squinted toward the area from where the noise had come. He lost his place, stammered, and seemed dazed for a moment. Then he recovered and tried to go on.

But now a new chant was drifting in the air, all around the central square, growing louder all the time: "Timişoara! Timişoara!" The massacre of civilians in the extreme western corner of Transylvania had stirred the consciences of people in the Romanian capital, 400 miles away. The government organizers tried to signal their supporters to chant more loudly, to drown out the demonstrating students, but to no avail. Soon the chanting of a single word overwhelmed the entire square: "Timişoara!" The revolt in Bucharest had begun at last.

By now Ceauşescu seemed completely confused. His eyes darted from side to side. His words seemed stuck in his throat. Elena took a step forward, and in a voice picked up clearly by the television network's microphone she told her husband, "Promise them something. Talk to them!"[5] Ceauşescu attempted to continue his speech, but now all that could be heard were the whistles and jeers of the crowd below. The students were in firm control of the square. The pro-government demonstrators had either fled to their buses or had thrown down their flags and portraits and had joined the protesters.

The crowd pressed against the large iron gates of the Central Committee building. One of Ceauşescu's advisors approached him and whispered, "They're coming in," and tried to lead Ceauşescu back from the balcony. Frightened by the advancing crowd, the government camera operator jumped from his platform and ran for cover. The unsupervised camera spun around crazily before finally coming to rest. For several minutes, television viewers across Romania stared at a picture of the gray sky over Bucharest and the roof of the Central Committee building. All this time, however, Ceauşescu's microphone remained on, allowing Romanians to listen as the man once praised as the "Chosen Titan Among Titans" frantically tried to regain the attention of the crowd. "Hello," he shouted into the microphone before him, over and over again. "Hello, hello, hello!"

Then, suddenly, the screen went blank. When the broadcast resumed several minutes later, the whistling, hooting, and shouting of the crowd in the square all but drowned out Ceauşescu's final public words. "Let us all act to serve the people, independence, and socialism!"[6] he urged. Then he and Elena fled from the balcony back into the building.

▼ ▲ ▼

By nightfall the streets of Bucharest were filled with thousands of men and women demanding an end to the hated Communist regime. Ceauşescu immediately declared martial law and ordered army battalions to clear Gheorghiu-Dej Square. Using water cannons, tear gas, and rubber bullets, the army managed to force the protesters several blocks south to University Square.

Ceauşescu then summoned Defense Minister Milea and ordered him to use deadly force to restore order to the capital. Milea, however, declared that Timişoara was the last place that live ammunition would be used by the Romanian army against Romanian civilians. He refused to order his troops in Bucharest to open fire on the crowds. On Ceauşescu's order, a Securitate agent then shot Milea dead on the spot. Government-controlled news agencies were ordered to report that the defense minister had committed suicide. But Milea's "suicide" made it clear that Ceauşescu was no longer firmly in control.

By dawn the next morning, December 22, most Romanian army units had declared their support for the anti-Ceauşescu revolution. Crowds numbering in the tens of thousands were now gathered in front of the Central Committee headquarters, where the Ceauşescus and their closest associates were trapped. As the massive crowd battered at the entrance of his fortress, the dictator hurriedly telephoned party leaders across the country. Finally, Ceauşescu decided to flee to his estate at Snagov, about 20 miles north of Bucharest. From there he would go into hiding deep in the Carpathian Mountains until the Securitate brought the country back under control.

A short time later, a Securitate helicopter swooped low over the center of Bucharest and touched down on the roof of the Central Committee headquarters. Securitate agents loaded food, blankets, medical supplies, and weapons on board. The dictator and his wife, by now nearly paralyzed by fright and exhaustion, had to be carried to the helicopter as well. Three crew members and four bodyguards also boarded the craft just before the door was finally closed. Badly overloaded, the aircraft struggled to rise from its launching pad. It barely managed to clear the tall public buildings in the center of the city, but finally it gained altitude and rose, up and away, heading north. The thousands gathered in the square below shouted insults and shook their fists as the hated dictator fled the capital.

Ceauşescu's helicopter had just taken off when the revolutionaries finally gained access to the Central Committee building. Another group of demonstrators stormed the entrance of the adjoining National Library. A large bonfire was lit, and hundreds of volumes of the Ceauşescus' writings and speeches were thrown from the balcony into the fire below. A few blocks away, an antigovernment crowd also had gained control of the country's broadcasting center. Soon, images of a new revolutionary government were being televised across the nation and around the world. Murica Dinesco, a well-known poet long held under house arrest by the Ceauşescu government, was among

Protesters in Bucharest express their anger toward Romanian dictator
Nicolae Ceauşescu.

the first to appear, shouting "We've won! We've won!" exuber-
antly before the camera. A short while later, a Romanian army
general appeared in full dress uniform, confirming that the
army had joined the revolution and calling upon all Ceauşescu
loyalists to lay down their arms.

It was also announced that a "Front for National
Salvation" had been formed to govern the country until free
elections could be held. It soon became apparent that one
man in particular, Ion Iliescu, wielded the most influence.
Earlier in his career, Iliescu had studied in Moscow, where he
had counted Mikhail Gorbachev as a close friend. Later, he

had served as one of Ceauşescu's most powerful advisors, but had parted company with the dictator during the 1970s. While the Front for National Salvation offered an alternative to Ceauşescu, many were concerned that there were few representatives of Romania's non-Communist opposition in the country's new government.

For the next two days, fierce fighting raged in the capital as the hastily organized revolutionaries struggled to stand up to attacks by the thousands of well-trained Securitate troops who remained loyal to Ceauşescu. On Saturday, December 23, General Iulian Vlad, head of the Securitate, appeared on national television to announce that he too was joining the revolution. He ordered all Securitate forces to surrender at once. In spite of Vlad's announcement, however, the Securitate stepped up its assault. Later it was discovered that Vlad was in actuality a pro-Ceauşescu spy, supplying the Securitate with critical information about the plans of the revolutionary government. When his real intentions were unmasked, Vlad was immediately placed under arrest.

▼ ▲ ▼

Meanwhile, the hunt for the Ceauşescus continued. Once he had safely landed at Snagov, the Conducator tried to decide where to go next. Elena kept busy packing for their escape and ordered a maid to fill nine suitcases with blankets, linens, and clothing. A little more than an hour later, the Ceauşescus boarded their helicopter once again, and the dictator ordered the pilot to fly to Tirgovişte, a large industrial center 50 miles to the north. However, shortly after taking off, the pilot managed to convince Ceauşescu that the helicopter was about to explode. Nervously the dictator ordered him to land at a nearby government airfield. From there, the Ceauşescus and their bodyguards hijacked a car from a local doctor. When it ran out of gas just a short way down the road, they quickly commandeered another. Finally, after a long ride, they arrived at a deserted agricultural college near Tirgovişte.

Now far away from the lavish accommodations to which he had become accustomed, Ceauşescu paced the floor of an empty dormitory. Time and again, he would check his watch, walk to the windows, and stare up into the sky. Later, some claimed that the dictator's watch was, in fact, transmitting a radio signal to the Securitate, informing them of his whereabouts. Ceauşescu was confident that when his secret police knew his location, they would come immediately to rescue him.

However, before the Securitate could determine the whereabouts of the Ceauşescus, they were discovered by forces of the Romanian army and placed under arrest. They were driven first to a nearby army barracks, but when it came under attack by Securitate forces, Ceauşescu and his wife were loaded into an army tank and driven for hours around the countryside.

Within the governing National Salvation Front, there was already disagreement over how to deal with the Ceauşescus. While some members believed that the despised couple should be brought back to Bucharest and given a public trial, a majority within the new government insisted that the pair be executed as soon as possible. Securitate forces in Bucharest were gaining ground in their struggle to regain control of the capital's airport and the national broadcasting center. Many believed that the Securitate would continue to fight as long as they believed the Ceauşescus were still alive. In time, they might eventually be able to overthrow the revolutionary government. Word was quickly relayed to the army units in Tirgovişte: The Ceauşescus must be eliminated.

▼ ▲ ▼

On December 25, 1989, Nicolae and Elena Ceauşescu were placed on trial before a makeshift military tribunal at Tirgovişte. They were charged with genocide against the Romanian people. Their reign of terror had caused the deaths of 60,000 Romanians, the prosecutor charged.

Ceauşescu defiantly refused to recognize the court's authority over him. "I am the president of Romania and the commander in chief of the Romanian army," he raged. He demanded to be placed on trial before a session of the Romanian Grand National Assembly.

The prosecuting attorney pressed on. The country had nothing to eat, no heating, no electricity. Children were dying. Yet the Ceauşescus lived in luxurious palaces. The Ceauşescus held lavish parties on their country estates. Yet children could not even buy a single piece of candy. "Why did you ruin the country?" the prosecutor asked. "Why did you export everything? Why did you make the people starve?"

Then the prosecutor turned on Elena. Did she know about the genocide in Timişoara, the lawyer asked, or was she just a scientist, concerned only with the fine points of chemistry? Quickly, Ceauşescu moved to defend his wife. "Her scientific papers were published abroad!" he shouted. "And who wrote the papers for you, Elena?" the prosecutor shot back. Finally, Elena exploded: "Such impudence!" she shrieked. "I am a member and the chairwoman of the Academy of Sciences. You cannot talk to me in such a way!"

But the prosecutor continued. "That is to say," he asked, "as a deputy prime minister you did not know about the genocide?"

"She was not *a* deputy prime minister," the Conducator interrupted, "but the *first* deputy prime minister!"

After the questioning of the Ceauşescus was completed, it took only a few minutes for the presiding judge to announce the verdict: guilty on all counts. The sentence was to be death by firing squad—to be carried out immediately.[7]

When the unit commander asked for volunteers to execute the couple, soldiers began fighting among themselves for the "privilege" of shooting the Ceauşescus! Finally a lottery was set up, and the "winners" were allowed to join the firing squad.

Late in the evening of December 25, 1989, as families across Romania celebrated Christmas openly for the first time in decades, Nicolae and Elena Ceauşescu were bound, gagged, blindfolded, and placed against a wall behind the army barracks in Tirgovişte. A commander gave the order to fire, and in an instant, their bodies fell to the ground, pierced by hundreds of rounds of automatic weapon fire. Then the night was silent.

Several hours later, the Ceauşescus' execution was announced, and pictures of their bullet-riddled bodies were broadcast over and over again on national television. Romania exploded in joy and celebration. "The anti-Christ died on Christmas Day!" some rejoiced. Others cheered, "Dracula and his bride are dead at last!"

With the death of their leader, the Securitate forces realized that their cause was lost. Fighting in the capital soon died down, and the last pockets of resistance in the countryside were quickly put down. In Bucharest, Timişoara, and other cities, candles of remembrance were lit for those who had died in the fight against the dictatorship. According to most reliable sources, the Romanian revolution had cost the lives of nearly 2,000 people.

From Transylvania in the west to the Black Sea in the east, Romanians cheered the downfall of the hated Ceauşescu regime. But when their holiday celebrations were over, many began to feel less than hopeful about their country's future. Were Ion Iliescu and the other leaders of the new government truly interested in democratic change, or did they seek merely the continuation of the Communist system, though in a somewhat less extreme form? Nicolae Ceauşescu had ruled Romania for almost a quarter of a century. Many now feared that it would take almost as long to heal the damage he had done.

chapter 10

New Year's Day, 1990

It had been a year for crowds gathering in public squares. These crowds had been angry, defiant, hopeful, and joyous. They had faced tear gas, water cannons, vicious dogs, and in some places they had been fired upon by soldiers using live ammunition. Yet they had stood firm, dedicated to their ideals and the task before them. And almost overnight, it seemed, they had changed the political face of the world.

Soviet leader Mikhail Gorbachev did not join the celebrating crowd as it gathered in Moscow's Red Square on that bitter cold New Year's Eve in 1989. He may already have retired for the night, before the new decade arrived. It had been a busy year for Gorbachev. He had traveled thousands of miles. Everywhere he went, it seemed, large crowds gathered to greet him, filling the air with chants of "Gorby! Gorby!" Just a few days previously, *Time* magazine had named him "Man of the Decade."

Within the Soviet Union, however, support for Gorbachev and his policies was declining steadily. The Soviet leader had succeeded in reforming his country's political system. He had instituted the first contested elections in the history of the Soviet Union, and he had convened a new national legislature, the Congress of People's Deputies, which would soon elect him as the nation's president. But all across the Soviet Union, people were more dissatisfied than ever. The Baltic republics of Latvia, Lithuania, and Estonia were threatening to break away from the union. The economy was beset with problems. Hard-liners within the Communist Party were protesting that Gorbachev had let things get out of hand and that the very foundations of Soviet Communism were now threatened. Many conservative Communists also blamed Gorbachev and his reform-minded foreign minister, Eduard Shevardnadze, for the "loss" of the USSR's former satellites in Eastern Europe.

On the other hand, reformers within the Congress were pushing Gorbachev to bring about even greater changes. Most observers had continued to underestimate Boris Yeltsin. Many, including Gorbachev, believed that support for Yeltsin would vanish as soon as the initial curiosity surrounding the Congress had passed and Yeltsin had become just one more deputy among several hundred others. However, as 1989 drew to a close, Yeltsin seemed as popular as ever, especially among those concerned with guaranteeing the interests of the Russian Republic within the union as a whole.

For the duration of the Congress, Gorbachev had also had to contend with Andrei Sakharov. Time and again, Sakharov criticized government policy or demanded that some specific reform be put in place. Just two weeks before, on December 12, Sakharov and Gorbachev had had their final confrontation. The old scientist had approached the podium of the Congress carrying a large cloth bag that he claimed contained telegrams and petitions from 60,000 Soviet citizens. From all across the USSR, Sakharov said, men and women had written to him demanding the repeal of Article Six of the Soviet constitution—the article that guaranteed the "leading role" of the Communist Party in the life of the nation. Sakharov urged the Congress to eliminate the party's leading role and establish the Soviet Union as a genuine multiparty democracy.

Gorbachev ordered Sakharov to take his seat, but Sakharov pushed on, just as he always did. "Sixty thousand signatures!" he exclaimed, just as his microphone went dead.[1] At Gorbachev's urging, the Communist majority in the Congress

Mikhail Gorbachev   Andrei Sakharov

then voted down Sakharov's request for a vote on repealing
Article Six.

On the evening of December 14, two days after this confrontation with Gorbachev, Andrei Sakharov returned to his
apartment after another long, heated session of the Congress of
People's Deputies. He ate a light supper, worked in his study for
several hours, and then went to bed, telling his wife, Elena
Bonner, that he was tired and not feeling very well. By the next
morning, Sakharov was dead of a heart attack. The Soviet
Union had lost one of its most persistent voices of reform.

The Congress assembled in special session several days later to
honor the memory of Andrei Sakharov. Gorbachev himself stood
as a honorary pallbearer by Sakharov's casket and delivered a
glowing tribute to the man with whom he had disagreed so many
times in the past. The cause of reform within the Soviet Union to
which the great scientist had dedicated his last ounce of energy
was now more alive than ever. It was to be only a matter of time
before many of the same reforms Sakharov had urged in his
final days became official government policy. Gorbachev realized that what had taken place in Warsaw, Budapest, Berlin,

Sofia, Prague, and even Bucharest would sooner or later also take place in Moscow—unless changes were made. Gorbachev knew that in a time of such momentous change, the Soviet people would not sit back and allow their leaders to do nothing.

Before the winter was over, Mikhail Gorbachev himself would be calling for the repeal of Article Six and an end to the leading role of the Communist Party of the Soviet Union. He would soon be saying that there should be free elections. No longer, he would declare, should the Communists fear the people in the way that "the devil is afraid of incense."[2]

▼ ▲ ▼

In less than a year, almost half a century of political history had been reversed. In one nation after another, a system that had seemed permanent had disappeared almost overnight. Once-powerful leaders had been disgraced, arrested, and, in one case, executed. A nation's historical villains were now transformed into its saints. Former political prisoners became presidents, prime ministers, and leading government spokespeople. A seemingly durable concrete wall and an impenetrable iron curtain that had once separated East from West were pulled to the ground.

And when the dust from the fallen barriers of Communism had settled, the world was changed. The Cold War drew to a close, and Europe was united once again. But soon, too, the initial joy and euphoria at Communism's fall gave way, and the massive challenges that still lay ahead became clear.

In China, the Communist government of Premier Li Peng still had a firm hold on power. Although Western governments had loudly condemned the bloody crackdown on the student demonstrators in Tiananmen Square, the Chinese government had quickly put down all opposition within China. Leading opposition figures were sentenced to long terms in prison, and silence settled over the land.

In Poland and Hungary, men and women who had spent much of their lives opposing the Communist government now faced a far different set of challenges. Representatives of the Solidarity movement formed a majority of Poland's government, but many Poles were not happy about the continued influence of Communists within the leadership of the country, especially the presence of General Wojciech Jaruzelski as Poland's president. In addition, the country's economy was in trouble, and the leaders of Solidarity held different opinions on what course of action to pursue. There was even evidence of a widening gap between Solidarity's chief leader, Lech Walesa, and the country's prime minister, Tadeusz Mazowiecki.

In Hungary, non-Communists were expected to win easily in elections scheduled for March 1990. Many believed that as a result of these elections, Hungary would emerge with the first completely non-Communist government in Eastern Europe. However, this government too would face immense economic problems: high unemployment, rapidly rising prices, and the highest foreign debt in all of Europe.

Soon after the opening of the Berlin Wall in November 1989, many people, both in the East and in the West, began to press for the reunification of Germany. The reform Communists who had taken over the leadership of the German Democratic Republic after the fall of hard-liner Erich Honecker were unable to slow the rush toward reunification. Free elections in East Germany were also set for March 1990, and it seemed increasingly probable that the political parties favoring unification with West Germany were headed for an overwhelming victory.

As the New Year came to Romania, joyful crowds filled the streets, still celebrating the fall of the Ceauşescu dictatorship just days before. But the tone of demonstrations in the streets of Bucharest and other large cities would change over the winter of 1990. Gradually, many Romanians came to doubt whether the country's new president, Ion Iliescu, was genuinely committed to democracy. Many Romanians believed that too

East German demonstrators carry a poster displaying a reunited Germany.

many of Ceauşescu's former supporters were still holding high positions in the Romanian government, economy, and armed services. Many feared that the Romanian revolution had been "stolen" by Communists who were now only pretending to be democratic reformers.

Although thousands of happy demonstrators crowded the streets of Czechoslovakia's capital, Prague, on New Year's Day, 1990, they would soon face the challenges of their nation's new reality. That very day in fact many Czechs and Slovaks were at home, gathered in front of television sets to hear the first official address of their new president, Václav Havel, who had assumed office just three days before.

"My people, your government has returned to you," Havel told his fellow citizens, But, he reminded them, the road ahead would not be easy. "Our country is not flourishing," Havel said. And then he listed, one after another, the problems that Communism had brought with it:

> *The enormous creative and spiritual potential of our nations is not being used sensibly. Entire branches of industry are producing goods which are of no interest to anyone, while at the same time we lack the things we need. A state which calls itself a workers' state humiliates and exploits workers. Our obsolete economy is wasting the little energy we have available. A country that once could be proud of the educational level of its citizens spends so little on education that it ranks as the seventy-second in the world. We have polluted our soil, our rivers and forests, bequeathed to us by our ancestors, and we have today the most contaminated environment in Europe. Adult people in our country die earlier than in most other European countries.*[3]

But even worse than all of these problems, Havel maintained, was the "contaminated moral environment" that Communism had created. People no longer trusted one another. They had forgotten how to tell the truth. They thought only of themselves. They had given up their faith in the future. But now, Havel declared, they had the chance once again to accept responsibility and to build Czechoslovakia into an independent, free, democratic, prosperous, and socially just republic. If the people of Czechoslovakia so chose, Havel insisted, their nation could become a beacon that would "radiate love, understanding, the power of the spirit and of ideas " to the entire world.[4]

As the new president offered these words of inspiration, he pointed to the lessons of the past and tried to apply them to the problems the nation might face in the future. Some of the difficulties were already clear. Others, such as the growing discontent of people in the eastern region, Slovakia, who would begin to question whether they should remain united with the Czechs, would only surface in time.

Havel was not the only one who spoke of the lessons of the past and hopes for the future as a new decade dawned over Eastern Europe. The church bells that rang in the New Year in Bulgaria's capital, Sofia, could barely be heard over the music of the once-forbidden rock-and-roll bands that also sounded in the city's central square.

"Communism, go away!" the Bulgarian rock musician Vasil Georgiev sang. "Children, sleep well again at last":

> *The soil is state property, the fields are poisoned,*
> *the water is polluted, the soil is depressed...*
> *Hair is cut short, beards are shaved,*
> *Chains on the legs, but now the world is changing...*
>
> *Communism, go away!*
> *Children, sleep well again at last.*
>
> *They separated us from the world, accused us of*
> *sub-version.*
> *They beat us at the police stations, and pinned*
> *medals on themselves.*
> *They hid themselves in palaces, built prison camps,*
> *and twisted history, but now the world is changing...*
>
> *Communism, go away!*
> *Children, sleep well again at last.*[5]

"Chestita Svoboda!" sang another Bulgarian rock band. "Chestita Svoboda! Congratulations, Freedom!" And as though describing the men and women who had changed the face of the world over the past year, the song continued:

> *Men, women, children with glowing faces*
> *I see all around me today,*
> *Hugging and kissing each other, saying without fear:*
> *May it flow like water!*
> *Chestita Svoboda! Congratulations, Freedom!*
>
> *From now on, we can be brothers again.*
> *Life is so short, let us never go back.*
> *People, rejoice, proudly wave the flag!*
> *May it flow like water!*
> *Chestita Svoboda! Congratulations, Freedom!*[6]

No one claimed that the fall of Communism in Eastern Europe would guarantee an easy life for the people of those lands. No one denied that difficult problems still lay ahead. But to people who had lived in a totalitarian nightmare for so long, a new day had finally come. And though the days that beckoned might be hard, the people of Central and Eastern Europe could at least now face the future as free men and women once again.

Glossary

Allies France, Great Britain, the Soviet Union, the United States, and the nations that sided with them against the Axis forces during World War II.

capitalist Referring to an economic system in which property is owned by private individuals or groups and the free market forces of supply and demand are the determining factors.

coalition In politics, a group composed of members of two or more political parties who have joined forces to achieve common objectives.

Communism An economic and political system in which all property is owned by the state and the society is placed under the control of a single (Communist) party.

conservative An individual who is slow to embrace change or who is satisfied in keeping affairs the way they are.

dissident An individual who speaks out in opposition to those in power. The term generally refers to those who opposed their nations' Communist governments.

dogmatist An individual who believes that the doctrines of a particular philosophy must be applied strictly.

fascist Referring to a political system characterized by a strong central government. The rights of opposition parties and individuals are severely limited.

liberalism Belief in the desirability of change or reform in a system or institution.

martial law Temporary rule by the military during a state of emergency declared by the government. Political rights are suspended and military troops are used to enforce the law.

Nazism The political system that, under Adolf Hitler, ruled Germany from 1933 to 1945. Its policies included a buildup in the German military; the annihilation of Jews, gypsies, and other groups; and the establishment of German supremacy over all Europe.

parliamentary democracy A political system in which voters elect representatives to a legislature (or parliament). The legislators in turn decide who will be the leader of the government.

revisionism A form of Communism under which leaders apply political doctrines according to the changing conditions in a particular nation.

socialism An economic and social system in which all property is owned in common for the good of the whole society.

Stalinism A strict form of Communism, under which the rule of the Communist party leadership is tightly maintained and opposing viewpoints are severely repressed.

1989:
A Time Line

February 6   Round Table talks begin in Warsaw between
Poland's Communist government and the
Solidarity movement.

March 26   Elections are held across the Soviet Union to
choose representatives to the Congress of
People's Deputies. Opposition candidates take
nearly 400 of the 2,250 seats, and nationalist
candidates score strong victories in the Ukraine
and the three Baltic republics.

April 7   The Polish Round Table concludes with an
agreement to hold free elections in June.

April 18   The death of Chinese Communist reformer Hu
Yaobang unleashes massive protests in Beijing.
Within a week, hundreds of thousands of pro-
democracy students are in control of Tiananmen
Square in the center of the Chinese capital.

May 2   The Hungarian government begins to remove
barbed-wire fences along its border with
Austria.

May 14   Mikhail Gorbachev arrives in Beijing for talks
with Chinese leaders.

May 25   The first session of the Congress of People's
Deputies opens in Moscow.

June 4   Thousands are killed as China's Communist
government moves forcibly against demonstrators in Tiananmen Square. Solidarity scores an
overwhelming victory in Poland's elections.

June 16   At a massive public funeral in Budapest, Imre
Nagy and other leaders of the 1956 Hungarian
uprising are reburied.

August 24	Solidarity's Tadeusz Mazowiecki becomes prime minister of Poland's government—the first non-Communist government in the history of the Eastern Bloc.
September 10	Hungary opens its border with Austria, allowing thousands of East Germans to flee to West German embassies.
October 8	The central committee of the governing Hungarian Socialist Workers Party votes to disband the party.
October 9	Following a visit by Soviet leader Gorbachev to East Berlin, massive demonstrations break out against East German Communist leader Erich Honecker.
October 18	Egon Krenz replaces Honecker as head of the East German Communist party.
November 9	The East German government lifts all travel restrictions to the West, thus making the Berlin Wall obsolete. Following massive demonstrations in the streets of the Bulgarian capital, Sofia, Bulgarian Communist Party leader Todor Zhivkov resigns.
November 17	Czechoslovak security units move forcibly against demonstrators in Wenceslas Square in Prague, killing one and injuring perhaps hundreds.
November 19	Thousands gather in Wenceslas Square to protest the actions of the police. Civic Forum is formed to coordinate the protests. Czechoslovakia's "Velvet Revolution" begins.

November 27	A massive general strike brings Czechoslovakia to a virtual standstill. The Communist government agrees to enter into negotiations with the opposition.
December 3	Egon Krenz resigns in East Germany; a reform-minded Communist government assumes power.
December 10	A coalition government made up of both opposition and Communist members takes power in Czechoslovakia.
December 14	Andrei Sakharov, leader of the Soviet opposition, dies at his home in Moscow.
December 15	Thousands riot in the streets of the Transylvanian city Timişoara in protest against the policies of the hardline Communist government of Nicolae Ceauşescu.
December 22	Ceauşescu flees the Romanian capital, Bucharest. A "Front for National Salvation" is formed to run the country.
December 23	Ceauşescu and his wife, Elena, are captured by troops loyal to the revolution.
December 25	Following a makeshift trial, Nicolae and Elena Ceauşescu are executed by firing squad.
December 28	Václav Havel is elected president of Czechoslovakia.

Chapter Notes

Chapter 1
1. *New York Times*, December 11, 1988, 19.
2. Timothy Garton Ash, *The Magic Lantern: The Revolution of '89 Witnessed in Warsaw, Budapest, Berlin, and Prague* (New York: Random House, 1990), 16.

Chapter 2
1. Lech Walesa, *The Struggle and the Triumph: An Autobiography* (New York: Arcade Publishing, 1992), 167–168.
2. Ibid., 168.
3. *New York Times*, February 7, 1989, 3.
4. Ibid., 3.
5. *New York Times*, May 24, 1989, 4.
6. *New York Times*, August 18, 1989, 1.

Chapter 3
1. Andrei Sakharov, *Memoirs* (New York: Alfred A. Knopf, 1990), 615.
2. Dusko Doder and Louise Branson, *Gorbachev: Heretic in the Kremlin* (New York: Penguin Books, 1991), 404.
3. Hedrick Smith, *The New Russians* (New York: Avon Books, 1991), 470–471.

Chapter 4
1. Doder and Branson, *Gorbachev*, 364.
2. *New York Times*, January 1, 1989, IV, 1.
3. Adam Platt, "Abrupt Ouster in Peking—Deng's Brush with Disorder," *Insight*, February 9, 1987, 30.
4. Bernard Gwertzman and Michael T. Kaufman, eds., *The Collapse of Communism* (New York: Times Books, 1990), 41.
5. *New York Times*, May 19, 1989, 10.

6. *New York Times*, May 20, 1989, 1.
   Also, Harrison E Salisbury, *Tiananmen Diary: Thirteen Days in June* (Boston: Little, Brown and Company, 1989), 5.
7. *New York Times*, May 21, 1989, 1.
8. Ibid., 17.
9. *New York Times*, June 5, 1989, 10.

Chapter 5

1. Noel Barber, *Seven Days of Freedom: The Hungarian Uprising, 1956* (New York: Stein and Day, 1974), 49.
2. Vladimir Tismaneanu, *Reinventing Politics: Eastern Europe from Stalin to Havel* (New York: The Free Press, 1992), 80.
3. Garton Ash, *The Magic Lantern*, 50.
4. Barber, *Seven Days of Freedom*, 231.
5. Garton Ash, *The Magic Lantern*, 59.

Chapter 6

1. Garton Ash, *The Magic Lantern*, 68.
2. Mark Frankland. *The Patriots' Revolution: How Eastern Europe Toppled Communism and Won Its Freedom* (Chicago: Ivan R. Dee, 1992), 226.
3. *New York Times*, October 19, 1989, 1.
4. *New York Times*, December 18, 1989, 14.

Chapter 7

1. *New York Times*, November 28, 1990, 6.
2. *New York Times*, November 11, 1989, 1.

Chapter 8

1. Garton Ash, *The Magic Lantern*, 80.
2. Ibid., 96.
3. *New York Times*, December 5, 1989, 14.
4. *New York Times*, December 30, 1989, 10.
5. Garton Ash, *The Magic Lantern*, 78.

Chapter 9

1. Erland Clouston, "The Turn of the Screws," *The Guardian*, August 22, 1988, reprinted in Hungarian Human Rights Foundation, "Bucharest's Intensified Campaign of Cultural Genocide against the 2.5 Million Hungarians of Rumania: Selected Press Clippings," October 13, 1988.
2. *Bangor Daily News*, January 11, 1990, 8.
3. Ibid., 8.
4. Bruce W. Nelan, "Slaughter in the Streets," *Time*, January 1, 1990, 36.
5. Edward Behr, *Kiss the Hand You Cannot Bite: The Rise and Fall of the Ceauşescus* (New York: Villard Books, 1991), 4.
6. *New York Times*, January 7, 1990, 15.
7. Ion Mihal Pacepa, *Red Horizons: The True Story of Nicolae and Elena Ceauşescu's Crimes, Lifestyle, and Corruption* (Washington, D.C.: Regnery Gateway, 1990), 427–437.

Chapter 10

1. Hedrick Smith, *The New Russians*, 509.
2. Robert G. Kaiser, *Why Gorbachev Happened: His Triumphs, His Failure, and His Fall* (New York: Simon and Schuster, 1992), 317.
3. Václav Havel, "Playwright-Dissident Václav Havel Assumes the Presidency of Czechoslovakia," in *Lend Me Your Ears: Great Speeches in History*, ed. by William Safire (New York: W. W. Norton, 1992), 629.
4. Ibid., 632.
5. Derek Paton, "Another Rocker of the Revolution," Institute of Current World Affairs, Hanover, N.H., August 1990, 3.
6. Ibid., 4.

Selected Bibliography

Barber, Noel. *Seven Days of Freedom: The Hungarian Uprising,* 1956. New York: Stein and Day, 1974.

Behr, Edward. *Kiss the Hand You Cannot Bite: The Rise and Fall of the Ceauşescus.* New York: Villard Books, 1991.

Bornstein, Jerry. *The Wall Came Tumbling Down: The Berlin Wall and the Fall of Communism.* New York: Arch Cape Press, 1990.

Doder, Dusko, and Louise Branson. *Gorbachev: Heretic in the Kremlin.* New York: Penguin Books, 1991.

Frankland, Mark. *The Patriots' Revolution: How Eastern Europe Toppled Communism and Won Its Freedom.* Chicago: Ivan R. Dee, 1992.

Garton Ash, Timothy. *The Magic Lantern: The Revolution of '89 Witnessed in Warsaw, Budapest, Berlin, and Prague.* New York: Random House, 1990.

Goldman, Marshall I. *What Went Wrong with Perestroika?* New York: W. W. Norton, 1991.

Gorbachev, Mikhail. *Perestroika: New Thinking for Our Country and the World.* New York: Harper and Row, 1987.

Griffith, William E., ed. *Communism in Europe: Continuity, Change, and the Sino-Soviet Dispute.* Cambridge, Mass: M.I.T. Press, 1964.

Gwertzman, Bernard, and Michael T. Kaufman, eds. *The Collapse of Communism.* New York: Times Books, 1990.

Halle, Louis J. *The Cold War as History.* New York: Harper and Row, 1967.

Kaiser, Robert G. *Why Gorbachev Happened: His Triumphs, His Failure, and His Fall.* New York: Simon and Schuster, 1992.

Kaplan, Robert D. *Balkan Ghosts: A Journey Through History.* New York: St. Martin's Press, 1993.

Pacepa, Ion Mihai. *Red Horizons: The True Story of Nicolae and Elena Ceauşescu's Crimes, Lifestyle, and Corruption.* Washington, D.C.: Regnery Gateway, 1990.

Remnick, David. *Lenin's Tomb: The Last Days of the Soviet Empire.* New York: Vintage Books, 1994.

Rupnick, Jacques. *The Other Europe: The Rise and Fall of Communism in East-Central Europe.* New York: Pantheon Books, 1989.

Sakharov, Andrei. *Memoirs.* New York: Alfred A. Knopf, 1990.

Salisbury, Harrison E. *Tiananmen Diary: Thirteen Days in June.* Boston: Little, Brown, and Company, 1989.

Sheehy, Gail. *The Man Who Changed the World: The Lives of Mikhail Gorbachev.* New York: HarperCollins, 1990.

Smith, Hedrick. *The New Russians.* New York: Avon Books, 1991.

Stokes, Gale. *The Walls Came Tumbling Down: The Collapse of Communism in Central Europe.* New York: Oxford University Press, 1993.

Tismaneanu, Vladimir. *Reinventing Politics: Eastern Europe from Stalin to Havel.* New York: The Free Press, 1992.

Walesa, Lech. *The Struggle and the Triumph: An Autobiography.* New York: Arcade Publishing, 1992.

Yelstin, Boris. *Against the Grain: An Autobiography.* New York: Summit Books, 1990.

Index